Book Copyright, 1961, by Public Affairs Press,
419 New Jersey Avenue, S.E., Washington 3, D. C.

Printed in the United States of America
Library of Congress Catalog Card No. 61-11522

New Frontiers of the Kennedy Administration

THE TEXTS OF THE TASK FORCE REPORTS
PREPARED FOR THE PRESIDENT

PUBLIC AFFAIRS PRESS, WASHINGTON, D. C.

FOREWORD

These task force reports, prepared for the advice and information of the nation's chief executive, constitute an approximation of a blueprint for the United States in the years ahead. Written by President Kennedy's top advisors, they authoritatively indicate the terrain of the new frontiers.

Anyone who has a complacent attitude toward the critical problems now confronting the nation is likely to find these reports both disturbing and presumptuous. They are disturbing because they demonstrate that much is amiss in American life today and they are presumptuous because their basic premise is that much needs to be done and done soon.

Although it is hardly likely that the Kennedy administration will follow the task force reports in every detail, it is difficult to believe that the President would have authorized their preparation and publication if it was not his intention to implement them. To all reasonable indications, he sponsored these reports because he considered them essential to public understanding of his program and realization of its fulfillment. Even those who are critical of Mr. Kennedy recognize that his deeds follow closely upon his words. As is now amply evident, he plainly means what he says—as well as what he authorizes to be said under his auspices.

In view of the obvious usefulness and importance of these reports in the years ahead, they are printed herewith in full as authorized by Mr. Kennedy. While the texts of some have appeared in several newspapers, most of the reports are not readily available to the public. Of all the reports published herein only two have been printed in full by the government. The remainder—issued in mimeographed form at various times, in various ways, and through various channels—are for all practical purposes inaccessible to the public.

In publicizing highlights of the task force reports, the nation's newspapers have, of course, performed an invaluable public service, but if the American people are to be fully familiar with the nature of the President's program it is essential that the complete texts of the reports be read, consulted, and understood.

Although this book has benefitted by official cooperation it does not constitute an official publication. Nevertheless, its contents belong in the public domain and can be quoted freely.

M. B. Schnapper

Editor, Public Affairs Press
Washington, D. C.

CONTENTS

1: SPACE FRONTIERS

I. Introduction

Activities in space now comprise six major categories: 1. Ballistic missiles; 2. Scientific observations from satellites; 3. The exploration of the solar system with instruments carried in deep space probes; 4. Military space systems. (Separate Classified Report); 5. Man in orbit and in space; 6. Non-military applications of space technology.

We rely on the first member of the list, ballistic missiles, for a large part of the retaliatory response to the Russian missile threat.

It is generally assumed by the American citizen that our vast expenditures of money and technical talent in the national space program are primarily designed to meet the overriding needs of our military security. The fact is, however, that the sense of excitement and creativity has moved away from the missile field to the other components of the list, and that missiles, long before they are in condition for us to depend upon them, are slowly being delegated to the category of routine management. Before we proceed in this report to discuss and support the important activities in the other five categories we wish to emphasize the hazard of failing to complete and deploy on time our intercontinental deterrent missiles.

In addition to the need to develop ballistic missiles to provide for our military security, there are five principal motivations for desiring a vital, effective space program. It is important to distinguish among them when attempting to evaluate our national space effort.

First, there is the factor of national prestige. Space exploration and exploits have captured the imagination of the peoples of the world. During the next few years the prestige of the United States will in part be determined by the leadership we demonstrate in space activities. It is within this context that we must consider man in space. Given time, a desire, considerable innovation, and sufficient effort and money, man can eventually explore our solar system. Given his enormous curiosity about the universe in which

Task Force: Jerome B. Wiesner, Chairman, Kenneth Belieu, Trevor Gardner, Donald F. Hornig, Edwin H. Land, Max Lehrer, Edward M. Purcell, Bruno B. Rossi, Harry J. Watters.

he lives and his compelling urge to go where no one has ever been before, this will be done.

Second, we believe that some space developments, in addition to missiles, can contribute much to our national security—both in terms of military systems and of arms-limitation inspection and control systems.

Third, the development of space vehicles affords new opportunities for scientific observation and experiment—adding to our knowledge and understanding of the earth, the solar system, and the universe. In the three years since serious space exploration was initiated the United States has been the outstanding contributor to space science. We should make every effort to continue and to improve this position.

Fourth, there are a number of important practical non-military applications of space technology—among them satellite communications and broadcasting; satellite navigation and geodesy; meteorological reconnaissance; and satellite mapping—which can make important contributions to our civilian efforts and to our economy.

Finally, space activities, particularly in the fields of communications and in the exploration of our solar system, offer exciting possibilities for international cooperation with all the nations of the world. The very ambitious and long-range space projects would prosper if they could be carried out in an atmosphere of cooperation as projects of all mankind instead of in the present atmosphere of national competition.

The ad hoc panel has made a hasty review of the national space program, keeping in mind the objective—to provide a survey of the program and to identify personnel, technical, or administrative problems which require the prompt attention of the Kennedy administration. We have identified a number of major problems in each of these categories, and they will be discussed in this report. It is obvious that there has been inadequate time to examine all facets of the program or to permit full consideration of the possible answers to many of the questions raised.

Because of the overriding necessity to provide more efficient and effective leadership for the program, the group has devoted a major portion of its time to this aspect of the space program. We will, however, indicate important scientific and technical problems which should be thoroughly examined as soon as possible. We have concluded that it is important to reassess thoroughly national objectives in the space effort—particularly in regard to man in space; space, science and exploration; and the non-military applications of space, in order to assure a proper division of effort among these activities. Space activities are so unbelievably expensive and people working in this field are so imaginative that the space program could easily grow to cost many more billions of dollars per year.

While we are now compelled to criticize our space program and its management, we must first give adequate recognition to the dedication and talent which brought about very real progress in space during the last few years. Our scientific accomplishments to date are impressive, but unfortunately, against the background of Soviet accomplishments with large boosters, they have not been impressive enough.

Our review of the United States' space program has disclosed a number of organizational and management deficiencies as well as problems of staffing and direction which should receive prompt attention from the new administration. These include serious problems within NASA, within the military establishment, and at the executive and other policy-making levels of government. These matters are discussed in the sections which follow.

II. The Ballistic Missile Program

The nation's ballistic missile program is lagging. The development of the missiles and of the associated control systems, the base construction, and missile procurement must all be accelerated if we are to have the secure missile deterrent force soon that the country has been led to expect.

While additional funds will undoubtedly be required to accomplish this, we believe that re-establishing an effective, efficient, technically competent management for the program is the overriding necessity.

Though the missile program is not ordinarily regarded as part of the space program, it is important to recognize that for the near future the achievement of an adequate deterrent force is much more important for the nation's security than are most of the space objectives, and that at least part of the difficulty in the management and execution of the program stems from the distraction within the Defense Department and in industry caused by vast new space projects. However, we have no alternative but to press forward with space developments.

III. Organization and Management

There is an urgent need to establish more effective management and coordination of the United States space effort. The new administration has promised to move our country into a position of preeminence in the broad range of military, cultural, scientific and civilian applications of satellite and other space vehicles. This cannot be done without major improvements in the planning and direction of the program. Neither NASA as presently operated nor the fractionated military space program nor the long-dormant space council have been adequate to meet the challenge that the Soviet thrust into space has posed to our military security and to our position of leadership in the world.

In addition to the difficulties and delays which the program has endured because of the lack of sufficient planning and direction, it has also been handicapped because too few of the country's outstanding scientists and engineers have been deeply committed to the development and research programs in the space field. In changing the management structure and in selecting the administrators for the effort, the need to make space activities attractive to a larger group of competent scientists and engineers should be a guiding principle.

The new administration has announced that it plans to use the National Aeronautics and Space Council for coordinating government space activities, for advising the President on policy on plans and on the implementation of programs. We believe that the space council can fulfill this role only if it is technically well-informed and, moreover, seriously accepts the responsibility for directing the conduct of a coherent national space effort. Particular care should be taken to insure the selection of a very competent and experienced staff to assist the Council.

Not only must we provide more vigor, competence and integration in the space field, but we must also relate our space requirements to other vital programs which support our national policy. We refer particularly to the missile needs, already mentioned, and to the continuing need for development and research in the field of aeronautics.

Each of the military services has begun to create its own independent space program. This presents the problem of overlapping programs and duplication of the work of NASA. If the responsibility of all military space developments were to be assigned to one agency or military service within the Department of Defense, the Secretary of Defense would then be able to maintain control of the scope and direction of the program and the Space Council would have the responsibility for settling conflicts of interest between NASA and the Department of Defense.

We are also concerned by the NASA preoccupation with the development of an in-house research establishment. We feel that too large a fraction of the NASA program, particularly in the scientific fields, is being channeled into NASA-operated facilities.

One important responsibility of NASA given little attention now in the organization, is that of providing for basic research and advanced development in the field of aeronautics . There is a general belief in the aviation industry that the national preoccupation with space developments has all but halted any advance in the theory and technology of aerodynamic flight. There is ample evidence to support the contention that the Russians and possibly the British, are surpassing us in this field and consequently in the development of supersonic commercial aircraft. We should make a substantial effort to correct this situation, possibly by getting some of NASA's aeronautical and aerodynamic experts back into the field of advanced aircraft research and development. Possibly, after careful investigation, the Space Council would prefer to stimulate this work by non-governmental arrangements, or by placing it entirely in another agency.

We believe that the work of NASA would be facilitated and the task of recruiting staff made possible if an outstanding expert was placed in charge of the direction and management of each of the following important areas of work:

    a. Propulsion and vehicle design and development
    b. The space sciences
    c. Non-military exploitation of space technology
    d. Aeronautical sciences and aircraft development

IV. THE BOOSTER PROGRAM

The inability of our rockets to lift large payloads into space is the key to the serious limitations of our space program. It is the reason for the current Russian advantage in undertaking manned space flight and a variety of ambitious unmanned missions. As a consequence, the rapid development of boosters with a greater weight-lifting capacity is a matter of national urgency.

Payload weight is currently limited by our dependence on modified military rockets as the primary boosters (Thor, Jupiter, Atlas). Current plans call for the first substantial increase in payload with the addition of the Centaur upper stage to the Atlas in 1962, followed by a second big step with the Saturn booster in 1965.

It is likely that a variety of new booster programs will be proposed in the near future, particularly for military projects. There are no fundamental differences in civilian and military requirements which are foreseeable now. If the national effort is to be focused and the very large expenditures are not to be distributed among an excessive number of booster programs, it is important that we maintain and strengthen the concept of a National Booster Program.

A number of problems may well arise in the National Booster Program. The present Mercury program, based on the Atlas, is marginal and if the Atlas proves inadequate for the job it may be necessary to push alternatives vigorously. The first possibility appears to be the Titan, although it has not yet demonstrated the reliability which is required. We should study the desirability of carrying out a Titan-boosted Mercury program in the event Atlas should prove to be inadequate.

The Centaur rocket involves an entirely new technology and is still untested. If difficulties develop in this program within the next three or four months we must act promptly to initiate an alternate.

Development of the Saturn-booster—a cluster of eight Atlas engines —should continue to be prosecuted vigorously. However, it would be dangerous to rely on Saturn alone for the solution to our problems, either in the long or short term, for two reasons:

a. It is intrinsically so complex that there is a real question whether it can be made to function reliably.

b. It represents a maximum elaboration of present technology and provides no route to further development.

Therefore, the development of a very large single engine should proceed as fast as possible so that it may be a back-up for the Saturn cluster and a base for future larger vehicle development. The present F-1 (1.5 million lb. thrust) engine development should be studied to be sure it is progressing fast enough and has enough promise of success to fill this role. If the technological step in going from the present 180,000 lb. thrust engines to 1.5 million lbs. is so big as to make success marginal, a parallel development of a somewhat smaller engine should be started.

The nuclear rocket program (Rover) presents an area in which some major decisions will have to be taken by the new administration. In principle the nuclear rocket can eventually carry heavier payloads much farther than any chemical rocket. Nevertheless, the technology is so new and the extrapolation from reactors developed now to sizes which would be useful in large rockets is so great that it is not clear how soon they will make an important contribution to the space program. The use of nuclear rockets will raise serious international political problems since the possibility that a reactor could reenter and fall on foreign territory cannot be ignored. A major technical and management review of the Rover program seems urgent.

Above all we must encourage entirely new ideas which might lead to real breakthroughs. One such idea is the Orion proposal to utilize a large number of small nuclear bombs for rocket propulsion. This proposal should receive careful study with a realization of the international problems associated with such a venture.

V. Science in Space and Space Exploration

In the three years since space exploration began, experiments with satellites and deep space probes have provided a wealth of new scientific results of great significance. In spite of the limitations in our capability of lifting heavy payloads, we now hold a position of leadership in space science. American scientists have discovered the great belt of radiation, trapped within the earth's magnetic field. American scientists have revealed the existence of a system of electric currents that circle our planet. Our space vehicles have probed the interplanetary space to distances of tens of millions of miles from the earth. They have shown that the earth is not moving through an empty space but through an exceedingly thin magnetized plasma. They have intercepted streams of fast-moving plasma ejected from the sun which, upon reaching our planet, produce magnetic storms, trigger off auroral displays and disrupt radio communications.

From these and other experiments, there is gradually emerging an entirely novel picture of the conditions of space around our planet and of the sun-earth relations. One of the important tasks of space science in the next few years will be a full exploration of the new field revealed by the early experiments. There is little doubt that such exploration will lead to further important discoveries.

Another scientific field, where space science promises an early and major break-through is that of astronomy. Until a few years ago, visible light from celestial objects, reaching our telescopes through the atmospheric blanket, had been the only source of astronomical information available to man. The only other portion of the spectrum capable of penetrating the atmosphere and the ionosphere is that corresponding to short-wave radio signals. In recent years, the development of radio telescopes has made it possible to detect these signals. Radio astronomy has enormously advanced our knowledge of the universe. By means of radio telescopes we can now "see" not only the stars, but also the great masses of gas between the stars; we can detect the high-energy electrons produced by cosmic accelerators located thousands or millions of light years away from the earth.

We are entitled to expect a similar and even perhaps a more spectacular advance the day that we shall have telescopes installed aboard satellites circling the earth above the atmosphere and the ionosphere. These instruments will be capable of detecting the whole of the electro-magnetic spectrum—from long-wave radio signals to gamma-rays.

A third major task of space science in the years to come will be the exploration of the moon and the planets. Scientists are planning to fly instruments to the vicinity of these celestial objects, and eventually to land them upon their surface. From the data supplied by these instruments they expect to obtain information of decisive importance concerning the origin and the evolution of the solar system. Moreover, there is the distinct possibility that planetary exploration may lead to the discovery of extra-terrestrial forms of life. This clearly would be one of the greatest human achievements of all times.

Our present leadership in space science is due to a large extent to the early participation of some of our ablest scientists in our space program—primarily as part of the International Geophysical Year—and to the fact that these scientists were in a position to influence this program. Another important factor was our initial advanage in instrumentation, which helped to offset our disadvantage in propulsion.

We must not delude ourselves into thinking that it will be easy for the U.S.A. to maintain in the future a prominent position in space science. The USSR has a number of competent scientists. It will be easier for them to catch up with us in instrument development than for our engineers to catch up with the Russians in the technique of propulsion. Thus we must push forward in space science as effectively and as forcefully as we can.

Our scientific program in space appears to be basically sound. However, to insure its success, the following requirements must be met.

1. In the planning of our space activities, scientific objectives must be assigned a prominent place.

2. Our space agency must insure a wide participation in its program

by scientists from universities and industrial laboratories, where our greatest scientific strength lies.

3. It must provide adequate financial support for the development and construction of scientific payloads.

4. It must exert the greatest wisdom and foresight in the selection of the scientific missions and of the scientists assigned to carry them out.

5. It must initiate immediately a research program in advanced instrumentation, so that we may be ready to exploit fully the capability of flying heavier and more complex payloads that we shall possess several years from now. Problems of automation, processing and transmission of information must be tackled by competent and imaginative research teams.

VI. Man in Space

We are rapidly approaching the time when the state of technology will make it possible for man to go out into space. It is sure that, as soon as this possibility exists, man will be compelled to make use of it, by the same motives that have compelled him to travel to the poles and to climb the highest mountains of the earth. There are also dimly perceived military and scientific missions in space which may prove to be very important.

Thus, manned exploration of space will certainly come to pass and we believe that the United States must play a vigorous role in this venture. However, in order to achieve an effective and sound program in this field, a number of facts must be clearly understood.

1. Because of our lag in the development of large boosters, it is very unlikely that we shall be first in placing a man into orbit around the earth.

2. While the successful orbiting of a man about the earth is not an end unto itself, it will provide a necessary stepping stone toward the establishment of a space station and for the eventual manned exploration of the moon and the planets. The ultimate goal of this kind of endeavor would, of course, be an actual landing of man on the moon or a planet, followed by his return to the earth. It is not possible to accomplish such a mission with any vehicles that are presently under development.

3. The acquisition of new knowledge and the enrichment of human life through technological advances are solid, durable, and worthwhile goals of space activities. There is general lack of appreciation of this simple truism, both at home and abroad. Indeed, by having placed

highest national priority on the Mercury program we have strengthened the popular belief that man in space is the most important aim
of our non-military space effort. The manner in which this program
has been publicized in our press has further crystallized such belief.
It exaggerates the value of that aspect of space activity where we
are less likely to achieve success, and discounts those aspects in which
we have already achieved great success and will probably reap further
successes in the future.

VII. Non-Military Applications of Space Technology — An Industry-Government Space Program

As the technical feasibility and reliability of man-made satellites
was demonstrated, many possible civilian uses for satellites emerged.
With no government support, various groups in private industry
have examined the field for areas of study and development and a
few substantial projects are already under way.

Industrial and governmental communications satellites appear
practical and economically sound. Communication satellites will
provide high quality and inexpensive telephone and general communication service between most parts of the earth. A by-product
of a communication satellite will almost surely be an international
television relay system linking all the nations of the world. On a
longer time scale it should be feasible to provide radio and television
broadcasting service via satellite-mounted transmitters. Such systems
would give the quality broadcast reception now only available in and
near urban areas to most of the inhabitants of the earth.

Satellites containing reliable beacons can be used to provide improved means of navigation for aircraft and ships at sea and can
greatly advance the field of geodetics.

Proper use of the information gathered by meteorological satellites
should greatly increase our understanding of meteorology. With more
knowledge of meteorology and with world-wide data frequently
available from the satellites, longer-range and more reliable weather
predictions should be possible. These projects, dreams a decade ago,
bridge areas of technical speciality in which this nation is unexcelled.
The United States has the most advanced communication system in
the world, with a vast scientific and technological base supporting the
communication industry. We are preeminent in the development of
our electronic skills in radio, television, telephone and telegraphy.
This entire industrial-scientific base is available to apply its art
through satellite systems to the civilian needs of the world.

The exploitation of a new area of industrial opportunity for civilian use is normally left by our government to private enterprise. However, in the case of these important space systems, the development investment required is so large that it is beyond the financial resources of even our largest private industry. Furthermore, the use of commercial space satellites will require physical support of government installations as well as financial support.

All of the civilian satellite projects listed here will have direct or indirect military usefulness as well. Furthermore, communication and navigation systems of the type envisaged would be extremely useful in implementing an inspection system which might accompany a disarmament agreement. For these reasons projects of the type proposed might well be undertaken in cooperation with the military services.

We recommend a vigorous program to exploit the potentialities of practical space systems. The government, through NASA or the Department of Defense, should make available the required physical facilities as well as any extraordinary financial support required to make the undertakings successful.

Organizational machinery is needed within the executive branch of the government to carry out this civilian space program.

SUMMARY OF RECOMMENDATIONS

1. Make the Space Council an effective agency for managing the national space program.

2. Establish a single responsibility within the military establishments for managing the military portion of the space program.

3. Provide a vigorous, imaginative, and technically competent top management for NASA, including: *a*: Administrator and deputy administrator. *b*: i. A technical director for propulsion and vehicles; ii. A technical director for the scientific program; iii. A technical director for the non-military space applications; iv. A technical director for aerodynamic and aircraft programs.

4. Review the national space program and redefine the objectives in view of the experience gained during the past two years. Particular attention should be given the booster program, manned space flight, the military uses of space, and the application of space technology to the civilian activities of the country.

5. Establish the organizational machinery within the government to administer an industry-government civilian space program.

2: DEFENSE FRONTIERS

INTRODUCTORY STATEMENT

Since its appointment on September 14, 1960, the Committee, within
the limits imposed by the time available, has attempted to bring up
to date various earlier studies of the administration and management
of the Defense Department and related defense agencies and organizations.

In the course of its consideration of possible changes in the Defense
Establishment, the Committee, in accordance with your instructions†,
has made use of the extensive materials on that subject which have
been developed during recent years through the work of Congressional
Committees and of private study groups.

Some of the proposals advocated by such Committees and groups
fall short of, while others would go beyond, the measures recommended by this Committee.

While thus taking advantage of the great body of source material
available to it in the area of defense management and administration,
the Committee has not met formally with others. Nevertheless,
individual members of the Committee have had the benefit, in arriv-
ing at their present conclusions, of the general thinking on many of
the matters dealt with in this Report of a number of former officials
in the Defense Department.

*   *   *

In any appraisal of the U. S. military posture one salient factor
stands out above the rest. That is the three-fold significance of
reaction time at this stage in history:

First is the unprecedented strategic value of time—the ability to
react instantly against aggression in this nuclear-space age.

In World Wars I and II our country had at least eighteen months
to build and mobilize its defenses.

Submitted by Senator Stuart Symington as chairman of the task force listed on
pages 20 and 21.

† As contained in release of September 14, 1960, attached hereto as Exhibit B.

If there should ever be a World War III, we would be fortunate to have eighteen minutes to react.

Second is the crucial time element in the United States v. Soviet arms race—the need for early selection among alternative weapons systems and for shorter lead times between conception and use.

Third is the effect of time on defense cost. Regardless of how much the people of this country spend, they cannot buy time. Yet we tend to forget the costly effect of building weapons which have become obsolescent as a result of delay.

Only by giving full recognition to these all-important time factors can the Defense Establishment of the United States be strengthened in a meaningful way.

*   *   *

BACKGROUND OF COMMITTEE RECOMMENDATIONS

The existing structure of the Department of Defense is still patterned primarily on a design conceived in the light of lessons learned in World War II, which are now largely obsolete.

The piecemeal amendments to the basic legislation effected in 1949 and 1958 and the "reorganization" of 1953 did not alter the essential character of the U. S. military organization, deployed on the basis of whether a military man travels on land, sea or air. Hence it can be truly said that since 1947 there has been no fundamental change in the scheme of organization of our armed forces.

Yet, during this period of nearly a decade and a half, the whole state of the art in military science has been revolutionized, as epitomized in the transitions to the jet, nuclear and space ages.

No longer is the prime mission of the military forces of the United States to prevail in a World War II-type of open warfare; now it is to insure the defense and survival of the nation in the current era of cold war and protracted conflict, with always the possibility of nuclear attack.

Changes of comparable magnitude have taken place in the international political conditions which constantly accentuate the military risks to which the United States is now subject.

Although two partial reorganizations of the Defense Department since 1952 failed to bring the organizational structure of the Department into line with the requirements of today's military conditions, the necessity for modernizing the defense organization has been widely recognized; and both the Administration and the Congress have been repeatedly urged to take further measures.

In 1958 the Rockefeller Brothers Report recommended major changes in the military establishment to remedy those central weaknesses in its structure which have contributed to the lag in U. S. weapons systems development versus that of the Soviets.

In 1959 Senator Cooper proposed a bill designed to make improvements in the administration and control of the Defense Department; and in 1960 Senator Symington introduced amendments to the National Security Act which would have effected further reorganization of the Defense Department.

It was in the light of such bipartisan moves that the Democratic Platform for 1960 called for "a complete examination of the organization of our armed forces," as a first order of business of the next Administration, and that Senator Kennedy asked this Committee to produce for him "a concrete program with specific proposals in the clearly defined field of its responsibility."

Throughout all proposals, past and present, to make more effective the Defense Department organization has run one central theme— the clarification and strengthening of the authority of the Secretary of Defense over the entire U. S. Military establishment.

There are some who believed, even prior to the 1958 amendments to the National Security Act, that existing legislation provided ample basis for the Secretary's authority. Others took a contrary view. It is the conclusion of this Committee that the doctrine of civilian control will be compromised as long as any doubts exist on this vital point.

Besides resolving any such remaining doubts, there are three major objectives to be sought in modernizing the present Defense Department structure:

First, there must be a shortening of the time factor in bringing new weapons systems from conception to utilization without duplication and wasted effort. Under the existing multi-layered structure it is only possible to reduce administrative—i.e., decision-making—lead time by crash procedures set up for key programs such as the Special Projects Office of the Navy now in charge of the Polaris program and the Ballistic Missile Division established by the Air Force to expedite the ICBM program. This *ad hoc* streamlining of weapons systems management inevitably slows up progress in other areas.

Furthermore, for today's advanced weapons, such as missiles, and tomorrow's possible new ones, such as space vehicles, there is no longer any validity in separating the development and production cycle into two parts. This has been the practice with World War II-type and other conventional weapons which, when developed, can be manufactured by production line techniques.

With the present need for concurrency in many stages of weapons systems management, and with the relatively limited number of any given advanced weapon that will be produced, rigid distinctions between Research & Development and Procurement & Production organizations are no longer needed, and their performance should be more closely coordinated in the interest of economy in time, money and motion.

Second, the predominance of Service influence in the formulation of defense planning and the performance of military missions must be corrected. At present, defense planning represents at best a series of compromised positions among the military services. Action by the Joint Chiefs of Staff takes place, if at all, only after prolonged debate, coordination and negotiation between the staffs of the three Service Chiefs in preparing them to represent the points of view of their Services in the Joint Chiefs of Staff.

No different results can be expected as long as the members of the Joint Chiefs of Staff retain their two-hatted character, with their positions preconditioned by the Service environment to which they must return after each session of the Joint Chiefs of Staff. Nor can the Joint Staff become fully effective in developing the basis for clear military judgments unless the present degree of influence exercised by separate Service thinking is sharply reduced.

In short, there is a clear need for defense interest rather than particular service interest.

Third, there must be more effective utilization of human effort and material resources in the Defense Establishment. This can only be achieved through a flexible organization conforming to the present day nature of military missions instead of traditional service concepts. Such a change in organization would tend to minimize the duplication and delay growing out of the present multiple layers of control and the overlapping among military programs and operations caused by steadily increasing inter-service rivalry in an effort to fulfill common missions.

No longer can this nation afford the luxury of letting each service strive to develop in itself the capability of fighting any future war by itself. The national resources available for our country's defense

effort are in limited supply, and we cannot afford such waste of either
manpower or funds.

*   *   *

RECOMMENDATIONS FOR DEFENSE DEPARTMENT REORGANIZATION

In order to accomplish the objectives mentioned above, the Com
mittee recommends the elimination of the present departmenta'
structure of the Army, Navy and Air Force, but would preserve the
military Services as separate organic units within a single Defense
Department. Such a step would do away with the present departmental Service Secretaries and their Under and Assistant Secretaries,
fifteen in all.

Certain of the defense reorganization proposals that contemplate
this change, such as the bills introduced during recent sessions of
Congress by Senator Cooper (S. 2728) and Senator Symington
(S. 2957), have made provisions for replacing the present Service
Secretaries with three new Under Secretaries of Defense for the
Army, Navy and Air Force. The Committee (including its Chairman) now believes, however, that, by perpetuating separate Service
secretariats, it will be more difficult to subordinate service interest to
national interest. The Committee therefore considers that it would
be wise to discontinue what is now a *dual system* of civilian control
as a result of interposing between the Secretary of Defense and the
Services themselves a set of Secretaries identified with each service.

Vesting directly in the Secretary of Defense the administration of
the Services would be consistent with the functional scheme of
military operations already now reflected in the unified commands,
would concentrate civilian control in the Department of Defense
at one level instead of two, would reduce the delays incident to
obtaining separate service department coordination and would
facilitate effective civilian direction of defense policy as distinct from
military operations.

Since the 1958 amendments of the National Security Act, the
chain of command runs from the President to the Secretary of Defense,
and, through the Joint Chiefs of Staff, to the Commanders of the
unified and specified commands. The only change in this operational
chain of command contemplated by the recommendations of the
Committee would be to substitute the Chairman of the Joint Staff
for the Joint Chiefs of Staff. Thus, orders to Commanders of unified
and specified commands would be issued by the Secretary of Defense

(or by the Chairman of the Joint Staff by authority and direction of the Secretary of Defense). These Commanders, in turn, would continue to have full operational control over the forces assigned to them.

Under the new structure proposed by the Committee the military services would retain their existing responsibilities for administrative and logistic support of the military Commands. The chain of command for such purposes, as distinguished from operational direction of the military Commands, would run from the President to the Secretary of Defense to the Chiefs of the Services rather than to the military departments through their Secretaries as at present. The effect of this one change in the chain of command for non-operational functions would be to shorten the chain—again, reduce delay—and to place the Chiefs of the separate Services (who would no longer serve on the Joint Chiefs of Staff) in direct line of command with the Secretary of Defense from whom their orders would issue.

The end result should be to accomplish what the Committee believes to be a major objective in any change of the Defense structure, namely, to make the Secretary of Defense the civilian official in the Department of Defense with unquestioned authority and control over *all elements* of the Department of Defense at *all levels*.

SPECIFIC RECOMMENDATIONS

A. *Strengthening Civilian Authority.*

1. The military Services would be retained, but the present departmental structure of the Army, Navy and Air Force would be eliminated. This in turn would do away with the present positions of Service Secretaries, Under Secretaries and Assistant Secretaries. The Services would remain separate organic units, albeit within a single department (as in the case today with the Marines), and subject to direction, authority and control of the Secretary of Defense.

2. There would be created two new Under Secretaries of Defense, one for Weapons Systems and one for Administration. Together with the Secretary and the Deputy Secretary, they would comprise the planned statutory appointees in the Department*. In addition,

---

* Mr. Marx Leva, while agreeing that there should be a drastic reduction in the number of Secretaries, Under Secretaries and Assistant Secretaries, believes that the Secretary of Defense needs the assistance of several additional Under Secretaries of Defense.

the Secretary of Defense may designate such civilian assistants as he deems necessary.

The seven existing offices of Assistant Secretary of Defense (in addition to the fifteen Service Secretarial offices) would be abolished. Their functions would be absorbed by Directorates set up under the two new Under Secretaries. This Directorate organization would be subject to change by the Secretary of Defense and should not be frozen into a pattern fixed by legislation.

3. The Under Secretary of Defense for Administration would be responsible for activities such as Financial Management (Comptroller), Personnel, Legal, Transportation and Communications, Legislative, Congressional Liaison, Public Information, and Health and Medical.

As rapidly as possible all military personnel would be subject to similar recruitment practices, rules for training and length of service, pay for comparable responsibilities, and flexibility of assignment and transfer within and among the services and the service schools and academies.

There would be unified direction and responsibility for all service schools and other military educational institutions .

4. The Under Secretary of Defense for Weapons Systems would be responsible to the Secretary for the complete cycle of weapons development, procurement and production; and also for construction and installations, including bases, housing and depots.

These activities would be managed through three Directorates, namely:

a. The Directorate of Research and Engineering, which would take over the functions now carried on by the present Director of Defense Research and Engineering, and in addition would be responsible for the following activities now located in the office of the Secretary of Defense: (1) The Science Advisory Board (formerly the Strategic Missiles Evaluation Committee). (2) The Research and Development Policy Council. (3) The Defense Science Board. (4) The OSD Ballistic Missile Committee.

The functions heretofore exercised by the Advanced Research Projects Agency would be absorbed in the new Research and Engineering Directorate.

b. The Directorate of Procurement and Production, which would be responsible for all procurement and production functions.

c. The Directorate of Facilities, which would be responsible for all activities regarding facilities and installations, including responsibility for the planning and construction of facilities for research and testing of weapons, industrial-type facilities for weapons production and maintenance, facilities for weapons operation and use—such as missile and space vehicle launching installations—and non-combatant facilities such as on- and off-base housing.

5. There would be created a Special Assistant to the Secretary of Defense for Arms Control who would serve as the Defense liaison in that area with the State Department; and also with other agencies as designated.

B. *Command of Military Operations.*

6. The Joint Chiefs of Staff would be reconstituted so the Chairman of the Joint Chiefs (to be redesignated Chairman of the Joint Staff) would be the principal military adviser to the President and the Secretary of Defense.

The Chairman would preside over a group of senior officers from all Services to be known as the Military Advisory Council. Each of such senior officers would be appointed by the President and would no longer have any functions or responsibilities in the Service from which he came and to which he would not return.

In addition, the Chairman would direct the Joint Staff enlarged commensurate with the added responsibilities of the Chairman.

7. Each of the Services would have a Chief who would not serve on the Joint Staff or the Military Advisory Council; and who would report directly to the Secretary of Defense.

8. There would be established the following unified Commands, the Commanders of which would report directly to the Chairman of the Joint Staff:

a. A Strategic Command, responsible for all strategic missions.

b. A Tactical Command, responsible for all limited and conventional defense missions.

c. A Defense Command, responsible for all continental defense missions.

Each of the above unified commands will include all personnel, equipment, and weapons systems required for the performance of its respective missions.

To the extent that any regional or area specified Commands would be required in addition to the above-listed unified Commands, their Commanders would also report directly to the Chairman of the

Joint Staff. Such Commands would be composed of units assigned from the unified Commands.

9. There would be established a unified Command in charge of the National Guard and Reserve elements of all of the Services. In addition to its other functions, this Command would be responsible for Civil Defense, and would report directly to the Chairman of the Joint Staff.

C. *Budgetary Procedures.*

10. The Secretary of Defense would be required to present to the appropriate Committees of the Congress a detailed explanation of the military requirements for all missions and Defense Department operations prior to the presentation of the Defense Budget to the Congress.

11. The appropriation of all defense funds would hereafter be made to the Secretary of Defense. Certain categories of the Defense Budget such as Research and Development and long-lead time procurement would be put on a multi-year instead of a one-year justification and appropriation cycle.

EXHIBIT A

See chart on page 23.

EXHIBIT B*

After consultation today with Senator Stuart Symington, Senator John F. Kennedy issued the following statement about the former's survey for Senator Kennedy of the organization and management of the nation's defense structure.

Senator Kennedy said that he had approved the appointment by Senator Symington of the following individuals to this Committee on the Defense Establishment:

Clark M. Clifford, Lawyer; Washington University (St. Louis); partner in Clifford and Miller; Special Counsel to President of the United States (1946-50); assisted in drafting National Security Act of 1947; U. S. Navy (1944-46); Naval Aide to President of the United States, 1946; Navy Commendation Ribbon.

Thomas K. Finletter, Lawyer and author; University of Pennsylvania; partner in Coudert Bros.; Special Assistant to Secretary of State (1941-44); Chairman, President's Air Policy Commission (1947-48); Secretary of the Air Force (1950-53); U. S. Army (1917-19).

---

* Text of announcement, "Committee on the Defense Establishment," released by Senator Kennedy, St. Louis, September 14, 1960.

Roswell L. Gilpatric, Lawyer; Yale University; partner in Cravath, Swaine, and Moore; Under Secretary of the Air Force (1951-53); member of Rockefeller Special Studies Project (1956-57); member of Advisory Panel to Joint Congressional Subcommittee on Military Application of Atomic Energy.

Fowler Hamilton, Lawyer; University of Missouri and Oxford University; partner in Cleary, Gottlieb, Steen and Hamilton; Special Assistant to Attorney General of the United States (1938-42); Chief of Enemy Branch of Foreign Economic Administration (1942-43); Chief Legal Counsel, U. S. Department of Justice (1945); General Counsel Senate Subcommittee on Airpower (1956); former member of Joint Intelligence staff of the Joint Chiefs of Staff.

Marx Leva, Lawyer; University of Alabama and Harvard University; partner in Fowler, Leva, Hawes and Symington; attorney in OPA (1941) and WPB (1942); served with U. S. Navy (1942-45), received combat citation; Special Assistant to Secretary of Navy (1947) and Special Assistant and General Counsel to Secretary of Defense (1947-49); Chairman, Civilian-Military Review Panel for Special Committee of U. S. Senate (1957).

Dr. Edward C. Walsh, Executive Director of the Committee, Economist; Lafayette College, Tufts University, and Ohio State University; university faculties (1930-42); Deputy Administrator of OPA (1946-47); Chief, Antitrust and Cartels Division in Japan (1947-50); Legislative Assistant in U. S. Senate (1953 to present).

Senator Kennedy said that he and Senator Symington had reviewed the scope, procedure and objectives of the work to be done by the Committee.

"The work of the Committee will be focused upon the administration and management of the Defense Department and related defense agencies and organizations.

"It will deal with such matters as the relationships between civilian and military, decision making in the Defense Establishment, the role of the Joint Chiefs of Staff, and the lag time in the introduction of new weapons.

"The Committee will not make another sweeping investigation or study of defense, military policies and resources such as has been so ably and thoroughly done in recent years by various House and Senate Committees, and by such private groups as the Gaither and Rockefeller Committees, the Council on Foreign Relations, the Foreign Policy Association, the Carnegie Corporation, the great universities, and others.

"Rather it will utilize their splendid work as its primary source for facts, analyses and informed opinion on the narrower field of defense management and administration with which it is called upon to deal.

"The principal problems are well known; and the information needed for their analysis is readily at hand.

"The crucial questions are those of judgment as to what changes should be made in the organization and administration of our defense agencies to eliminate or at least to diminish the present crippling effect of these problems upon our defense power.

"In this critical area of judgment the Committee will seek the views of each branch of the armed services and of defense industries and it will also seek the opinions and counsel of qualified and experienced civilians irrespective of their political affiliation or particular service backgrounds.

"We must improve the administration of our defense agencies and we must do so without delay. To that end, the Committee will make recommendations to me as to the measures, whether legislative or executive, that should be taken to achieve two primary and related objectives: (1) To obtain a defense adequate to protect the nation and to enable it to discharge its international responsibilities; and (2) To obtain such a defense within the framework of a free and solvent economic system.

"In short, I expect this Committee to produce for me a concrete program with specific proposals in the clearly defined field of its responsibility.

"At my request Senator Symington has undertaken to have his recommendations in my hands before December 31, 1960, so that the new administration could take such steps, including the recommendation of appropriate legislation to the Congress, as may be necessary to remedy present basic weaknesses in the administration and management of our national defense establishment."

DEPARTMENT OF DEFENSE

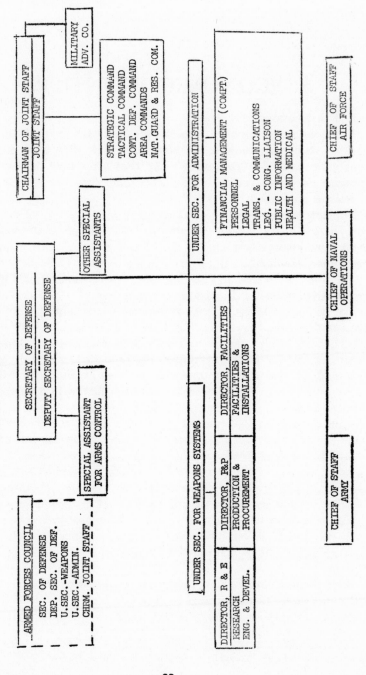

23

3: ECONOMIC FRONTIERS

I. The Economic Outlook

1. *Recession.* Economic experts are generally agreed that the nation's economy is now in a "recession." The slide since mid-1960 cannot be termed a "depression" like that after 1929, but so widespread a decline in production deserves more than the euphemism of a "rolling readjustment."

Prudent economic policy must face the fact that we go into 1961 with business still moving downward. This means that unemployment, now above 6 per cent of the labor force, may this winter rise more than seasonally. It means still lower profits ahead.

The fact of recession also has significant implications for the prospective Budget. It means a falling off of tax receipts from earlier estimated levels. This recession is wiping out the previously estimated Budget Surplus for the fiscal year ending June 30. Many experts now believe that as of today it is reasonable to forecast a deficit for this fiscal year, assuming only expenditures already authorized and in the absence of desirable new expenditures from an accelerated effort. Recalling the experience of the 1957-58 recession may be useful: due largely to the impact of a recession that everyone but the authorities admitted was then taking place, the announcement in early 1958 of a small fiscal 1959 Budget Surplus was actually followed by a final fiscal 1959 Budget deficit of more than 12 billion dollars! Not even the ostrich can avert the economic facts of life. He misreads the role of confidence in economic life who thinks that denying the obvious will cure the ailments of a modern economy.

No one can know exactly when this fourth postwar recession will come to an end. A careful canvass of expert opinion and analysis of the economic forces making for further contraction suggest this probability:

With proper actions by the government, the contraction in business can be brought to a halt within 1961 itself and converted into an upturn. Recognizing that many analysts hope the upturn may come

---

Credited solely to Dr. Paul A. Samuelson, Professor of Economics at M.I.T., who headed a task force on "economic conditions in the United States."

by the middle of the year but recalling how subject to error were their rosy forecasts for 1960, policy makers realize the necessity for *preparing* to take actions that might be needed *if* this fourth recession turns out to be a more serious one than its predecessors.

2. *Chronic slackness.* In economics, the striking event drives our attention from the less dramatic but truly more fundamental processes. *More fraught with significance for public policy than the recession itself is the vital fact that it has been superimposed upon an economy which, in the last few years, has been sluggish and tired.* Thus, anyone who thought in 1958 that all was well with the American economy just because the recession of that year bottomed out early was proved to be wrong by the sad fact that our last recovery was an anemic one: 1959 and 1960 have been grievously disappointing years, as the period of expansion proved both to be shorter than earlier postwar recoveries and to have been abortive in the sense of never carrying us back anywhere near to high employment and high capacity levels of operation. This is illustrated by the striking fact that unemployment has remained above 5 per cent of the labor force, a most disappointing performance in comparison with earlier postwar recoveries and desirable social goals.

If what we now faced were only the case of a short recession that was imposed on an economy showing healthy growth and desirable high employment patterns, then governmental policies would have to be vastly different from those called for by the present outlook. But this is not 1949, nor 1954.

Prudent policy now requires that we also combat the basic sluggishness which underlies the more dramatic recession. In some ways a recession imposed on top of a disappointingly slack economy simplifies prudent decision making. Thus, certain expensive programs that are worthwhile for their own sake, but that inevitably involve a lag of some months before they can get going, can be pushed more vigorously in the current situation because of the knowledge that the extra stimulus they later bring is unlikely to impinge upon a recovery that has already led us back to full employment.

The following recommendations try to take careful account of the fact that the recession slide is only the most dramatic manifestation of the grave economic challenge confronting our economic system.

II. Feasible Economic Goals

3. *Our economic potential.* Had our economy progressed since

1956—not at the dramatic sprint of the Western European and Japanese economies or at the rush of the controlled totalitarian systems but simply at the modest pace made possible by our labor force and productivity trends—we could have expected 1961 to bring a Gross National Product some 10 per cent above the $500 billion level we are now experiencing. With unemployment below 4 per cent, with overcapacity put to work, and with productivity unleashed by economic opportunity, such a level of activity would mean higher private consumption, higher corporate profits, higher capital formation for the future, and higher resources for much-needed public programs. Instead of our having now to debate about the size of the Budget Deficit to be associated with a recession, such an outcome would have produced tax revenues under our present tax structure sufficient to lead to a Surplus of around ten billion dollars; and the authorities might be facing the not unpleasant task of deciding how to deal with such a surplus.

4. *The targets ahead.* Looking forward, one cannot realistically expect to undo in 1961 the inadequacies of several years. It is not realistic to aim for the restoration of high employment within a single calendar year. The goal for 1961 must be (1) to bring the recession to an end, (2) to reinstate a condition of expansion and recovery, and (3) to adopt measures likely to make that expansion one that will not after a year or two peter out at levels of activity far below our true potential.

Indeed policy for 1961 should be directed against the background of the whole decade ahead. Specifically, if the American economy is to show healthy growth during this period and to average out at satisfactory levels of employment, we must learn not to be misled by statements that this or that is now at an all-time peak; in an economy like ours, with more than a million people coming into the labor force each year and with continuing technological change, the most shocking frittering away of our economic opportunities is fully compatible with statistical reports that employment and national product are "setting new records every year."

5. *Prudent Budget goals.* A healthy decade of the 1960's will not call for a Budget that is exactly balanced in every fiscal year. For the period as a whole, if the forces making for expansion are strong and vigorous, there should be many years of budgetary surpluses and these may well have to exceed the deficits of other years. Economic forecasting of the far future is too difficult to make possible any positive statements concerning the desirable decade average of such surpluses

and deficits. But careful students of sound economic fiscal policy will perhaps agree on the following:

(i) The first years of such a decade, characterized as they are by stubborn unemployment and excess capacity and following on a period of disappointing slackness, are the more appropriate periods for programs of economic stimulation by well-thought-out fiscal policy.

(ii) The unplanned deficits that result from recession-induced declines in tax receipts levied on corporate profits and individual incomes and also those that come from a carefully designed anti-recession program must be sharply distinguished from *deficits that take place in times of zooming demand inflation.* This last kind of deficit would represent government spending out of control and be indeed deserving of grave concern. The deficits that come automatically from recession or which are a necessary part of a determined effort to restore the economic system to health are quite different phenomena: they are signs that our automatic built-in stabilizers are working, and that we no longer will run the risk of going into one of the great depressions that characterized our economic history before the war.

III. The Constraints Within Which Policy Must Work

6. *Gold and the international payments.* Granted that the New Administration is preparing a whole series of measures to correct our balance of payments position, the days are gone when America could shape her domestic stabilization policies taking no thought for their international repercussions. The fact that we have been losing gold for many years will, without question, have to affect our choice among activist policies to restore production and employment. The art of statecraft for the New Administration will be to innovate, within this recognized constraint, new programs that promote healthy recovery.

It would be unthinkable for a present-day American government to deliberately countenance high unemployment as a mechanism for adjusting to the balance of payments deficit. Such a policy would be largely ineffective anyway; but even were it highly effective, only a cynic would counsel its acceptance. It is equally unthinkable that a responsible Administration can give up its militant efforts toward domestic recovery because of the limitations imposed on it by the international situation. What is needed is realistic taking into account of the international aspects of vigorous domestic policy.

7. *The problem of inflation.* Various experts, here and abroad, believe that the immediate postwar inflationary climate has now been

converted into an epoch of price stability. One hopes this cheerful
diagnosis is correct. However, a careful survey of the behavior of
prices and costs shows that our recent stability in the wholesale price
index has come in a period of admittedly high unemployment and
slackness in our economy. For this reason it is premature to believe
that the restoration of high employment will no longer involve problems concerning the stability of prices.

Postwar experience, here and abroad, suggests that a mixed economy
like ours may tend to generate an upward creep of prices *before* it
arrives at high employment. Such a price creep, which has to be
distinguished from the ancient inflations brought about by the upward
pull on prices and wages that comes from excessive dollars of demand
spending, has been given many names: "cost-push" inflation, "sellers"
(rather than demanders) inflation, "market-power" inflation,—these
are all variants of the same stubborn phenomenon.

Economists are not yet agreed how serious this new malady of inflation really is. Many feel that new institutional programs, other than
conventional fiscal and monetary policies, must be devised to meet
this new challenge. But whatever be the merits of the varying views
on this subject, it should be manifest that *the goal of high employment
and effective real growth cannot be abandoned because of the prob-
lematical fear that reattaining of prosperity in America may bring with
it some difficulties; if recovery means a reopening of the cost-push
problem, then we have no choice but to move closer to the day when
that problem has to be successfully grappled with.* Economic states-
manship does involve difficult compromises, but not capitulation to any
one of the pluralistic goals of modern society.

Running a deliberately slack economy in order to put off the day
when such doubts about inflation can be tested is not a policy open
to a responsible democratic government in this decade of perilous world
crisis. A policy of inaction can be as truly a policy of living danger-
ously as one of overaction. Far from averting deterioration of our
international position, a program that tolerates stagnation in the
American economy can prevent us from making those improvements in
our industrial productivity that are so desperately needed if we are to
remain competitive in the international markets of the world.

History reminds us that even in the worst days of the Great Depression there was never a shortage of experts to warn against all curative
public actions, on the ground that they were likely to create a problem
of inflation. Had this counsel prevailed here, as it did in pre-Hitler

Germany, the very existence of our form of government could be at stake. No modern government will make that mistake again.

IV. GENERAL POLICY RECOMMENDATIONS

8. *Introduction.* The two principal governmental weapons to combat recession and slackness are *fiscal* (i.e., tax and expenditure) policy and *monetary or credit* policy. In ordinary times both should be pushed hard, so that they are reinforcing rather than conflicting. These are not ordinary times. Until our new programs have taken effect, America does not have the freedom from balance of payments constraints that she enjoyed for the 25 years after 1933.

The usual balance between fiscal and monetary policies will have to be shifted in the period just ahead toward a more vigorous use of fiscal policy because of the international constraint. Some of the conventional mechanisms of credit policy may have to be altered to meet the new situation we face. While credit was made very easy in the 1954 and 1958 recessions in order to induce housing and other investment spending, a similar reduction of the short-term interest rate on government bills down to the one per cent level might lead in 1961 to a further movement of international funds to foreign money markets, thereby intensifying our gold drains. Because our monetary institutions are slowly evolving ones, the following recommendations deal less fully with monetary policy than the subject deserves in a full-scale study of stabilization.

9. *The need for flexibility.* Since experience shows that no one can forecast the economic future with pinpoint accuracy, the policy maker cannot plan for a single course of action; he must be prepared with a list of programs, reserving some on the list for the contingency that events in the early months of 1961 may turn out somewhat worse than what today seems to be the most likely outcome. The following recommendations of this report, therefore, fall into two parts.

First come those minimal measures that need to be pushed hard even if the current recession turns out to be one that can be reversed by next summer at the latest. Expansions and accelerations in expenditure programs that are desirable for their own sake, improvements in unemployment compensation, new devices that permit use of flexible credit policy within the international constraints and stimulus to residential housing are examples of measures that belong in our first line of defense and which are already seen to be justified by what we know about the recent behavior of the American economy. Now in January the wisdom of such policies can already be verified.

Second comes a list of other measures of expansion which represent sound programs to combat a sagging economy, but which are more controversial at this time. If we could read the future better, they might be just what is now needed. But given our limitations, it may be safer to hold such measures in reserve. As the months pass, and the February and March facts become available, we shall be in a position to know whether more vigorous actions are called for. Flexibility in decision making deserves emphasis: there is nothing inconsistent about asking for measures in March that one does not ask for in January, if events have provided us with new information in the meantime. The annual Budget should itself be a "living document." Just as Congress should begin to explore measures that will enhance the flexibility of tax rates by giving certain discretionary powers to the Executive, so should Congress itself be quite prepared to flexibly reverse its field in tax legislation when new economic conditions are recognized to call for new measures.

10. *Important warnings.* It is just as important to know what *not* to do as to know what to do. What definitely is not called for in the present situation is a massive program of hastily devised public works whose primary purpose is merely that of making jobs and getting money pumped into the economy. The Roosevelt New Deal inherited a bankrupt economy that was in desperate straits. Whatever the wisdom of anti-depression "make work" projects in such an environment, they are definitely not called for at the present time. There is so much that America needs in the way of worthwhile governmental programs and modern stabilization has so many alternative weapons to fight depression as to make it quite unnecessary to push the panic button and resort to inefficient spending devices.

Similarly, as was mentioned earlier, massive spending programs designed to undo in a year the inadequacies of several years do not represent desirable fiscal policy. Planned deficits, like penicillin and other antibiotics, have their appropriate place in our cabinet of economic health measures; but just as the doctor carries things too far when he prescribes antibiotics freely and without thought of proper dosage, so too does the modern government err in the direction of activism when it goes all out and calls for every conceivable kind of anti-recession policy. The golden mean between inaction and overaction is hard to define, and yet it must be resolutely sought.

Finally, it is worth repeating the warning against concentrating exclusively on ending a downward slide of activity and ignoring the suboptimal level at which the economy may then be operating. Even if this recession ended early in 1961, and even if its initial stages seemed to show a tolerable rate of improvement, that would not alone be enough to render unnecessary policies aimed to get us back to, and keep us at, high employment levels. Satisfactory growth is not something one procures by a once-and-for-all act; eternal vigilance, as with so many other good things, is the price that must be paid for good economic performance.

V. "First Line of Defense" Policies

11. *Expenditure programs.* Pledged expenditure programs that are desired for their own sake should be pushed hard. If 1961-62 had threatened to be years of over-full-employment and excessive inflationary demand, caution might require going a little easy on some of them. The opposite is in prospect. The following measures are not being advocated in the faith that they will help business from declining in the first months of the new year. Some of them will, at best, pay out money only after a considerable delay. They are advocated for their own sakes as builders of a better, fairer, and faster-growing economy. And even should their expenditures come into play after we have reversed the recession tide, they should be helpful in making the next recovery a truly satisfactory and lasting one.

(i) *Defense expenditures* ought to be determined on their own merits. They are not to be the football of economic stabilization. Nor, as was so often done in the past, ought they to be kept below the optimal level needed for security because of the mistaken notion that the economy is unable to bear any extra burdens. Certainly a recession drop in tax receipts should not inhibit vital expenditures any more than should the operation of artificial limits on the public debt. And they should certainly not be maintained at high levels merely for the purpose of substitution for other measures designed to keep employment high. On the other hand, any stepping up of these programs that is deemed desirable for its own sake can only help rather than hinder the health of our economy in the period immediately ahead.

(ii) *Foreign aid* is likewise to be determined by the need for development abroad. An increase in this program, skillfully tailored to take account of the international payment position, deserves high national priority in a period like this one.

(iii) *Education programs* including funds for school construction, teachers' salaries, increased loans for college dormitories should be vigorously pushed. Some of these could have an impact even within the calendar year 1961 itself.

(iv) *Urban renewal programs,* including slum clearance and improvement of transportation facilities, represent desirable projects that should come high on the policy agenda.

(v) *Health and welfare programs,* including medical care of the aged, increased grants for hospital construction, and continued large grants for medical research, are desirable even though some of them—such as health for the aged financed by social security—will not add at all to dollar demand in the near future.

(vi) *Improved unemployment compensation* is one of the most important of all the measures on this list from the standpoint of anti-recession action. The fairest and most effective step the Federal government can take to help fight the recession would be to expand unemployment compensation benefits. Such expenditures go to those who need them and who will spend the money promptly; they also go up at the right time and in the right place and will come down at the right time and in the right place. It is a sad fact, however, that the Nation's unemployment compensation system cannot possibly do the job it is expected to do. Under present arrangements, it was shown to be inadequate in the 1957-58 recession and it will be inadequate in the present recession as well.

For the immediate future, emergency legislation is needed to permit all states to continue paying unemployment benefits (perhaps at a stepped-up rate) for at least 39 weeks, regardless of the condition of their insurance reserves and even if they have not yet repaid the loans received to tide them over in 1958.

For the long pull, we need a system with basic Federal standards that will (a) cover employees in all firms regardless of size; (b) provide unemployment benefits of at least one half of the employee's earnings; and (c) extend the term of benefits to a minimum of 26 weeks in all states, supplemented by an additional 13 weeks during periods of high national unemployment. Federal standards are also needed to provide for adequate financing and solvency of the system. Consideration should also be given to the possibility of equalizing the burden of financing unemployment benefits among the states, and to varying the benefits in such a way that they will go up when unemployment in the nation as a whole is high and go down when unemployment is low. These measures would reinforce the stabilizing effectiveness of

the system in all stages of the business cycle and would eliminate the
need for hasty action during periods of emergency.

(vii) *Useful public works programs* should be accelerated to the extent feasible without disrupting their orderly execution. This applies
to Federal and federally-supported programs, such as (a) water resources, (b) highways, (c) post office construction, (d) public building construction by the General Services Administration, and (e) military construction. Prompt additional appropriations and authorizations by the Congress are needed in most cases. Opportunities for
speeding up authorized public works exist also at the State and local
levels. Cooperation of all levels of government strengthens an anti-
recession program.

(viii) *Highway construction programs* can be accelerated. Cement
capacity and labor availability is such as to make this a potent near-
term stimulant. An aggressive Federal highway program might involve any of the following measures: (a) relaxing contract controls
over State obligations, and assuring States their obligations will be
met; (b) authorizing repayable advance to the States to meet their
10 per cent matching requirements under the Interstate program; (c)
waiving the pay-as-you-go amendment if required to permit full apportionment of future Interstate authorizations and, if deemed necessary, increase these authorizations.

(ix) *Depressed area programs* are desirable both in the short run
and the long. The Douglas Report spells out needs in this matter and
makes comment unnecessary here.

(x) *Natural resource development projects*, including conservation
and recreation facilities, provide further examples of useful programs.

The above list does not pretend to be exhaustive. Certain other
expenditure measures could be added to a first line of defense program,
but enough has been said to indicate the nature of the needed actions.
The order of magnitude contemplated here might be in the neighborhood of $3-5 billion above already planned programs in Fiscal 1962
and does not involve the inflationary risks of an all-out anti-recession
Blitzkrieg. This does not purport to make up for the accumulative
deficiencies in those vital areas.

12. *Residential housing stimulus.* The last two recessions were
helped immensely by a successful program to make credit more available to residential housing. No experts could have predicted the anti-
cyclical potency that housing has shown in the postwar period. Already we have seen some easing of credit in this area, but such steps
do not seem this time to have been so successful in coaxing out a new

demand for home construction. There is perhaps some reason to fear
that less can be expected from the housing area in the year ahead.
Down payments are already quite low, as are monthly payments.
Vacancy rates, particularly in certain areas and for certain types of
housing have been rising. The age brackets that provide the greatest
demand for new housing are hollow ones because of the dearth of births
during the depression of the 1930's.

None the less, so great is the need for housing a few years from
now when the wartime babies move into the house-buying brackets
and so useful is the stimulation that a resurgence of housing could
bring that it would seem folly not to make a determined effort in this
area. In particular, loans for modernization of homes, which now bear
so high an interest rate, might provide a promising source for
expansion.

Many specific actions will be required. Mortgage rates might be
brought down to, say, 4½ per cent interest, with discounts on mortgages correspondingly reduced; consideration might be given to further
extended maximum amortization periods. The insurance fee for single
dwellings under FHA programs might well be reduced from ½ per cent
to ¼ per cent. The Federal National Mortgage Association (FNMA
or "Fannie May") could step up its mortgage purchasing program,
especially for high-risk mortgages lacking private markets. Housing
for the elderly is another program, desirable for its own sake. Measures
that tie in with urban renewal and college dormitories, as covered
above, also hold out promise.

Particularly because our international balance of payments inhibits
certain types of activistic monetary policy will it be necessary to push
hard on specific credit programs in the housing field. Innovation in-
genuity, and experimentation with new instrumentalities will be needed in this matter; it is not reasonable to believe that the patterns earlier arrived at are the last word in feasible programming.

13. *The role of monetary policy.* Were it not for the international
constraint, an economy that faced recession in the short run and which
had been falling below its potential for several years would naturally
call for a considerable easing of credit. Indeed a growth oriented program would entail a combination of low interest rates and widely
available credit with an austere fiscal program designed to create
Budget Surpluses large enough to offset any resulting overstimulation
of demand. But such a program must await a solution of our international economic difficulties that will free our hands in domestic
monetary policy.

The first order of business is to get nearer to high employment. Expansion by the Federal Reserve of bank reserves, in order to increase the supply of money and to stimulate investment spending, will naturally tend to lower short-term interest rates. But in view of the volatility of funds as between our money markets and those abroad which pay higher interest, we can plan only limited use of this conventional mechanism. New exploration is needed.

(i) In the days after the 1951 Accord when the lesson had to be learned that government bonds were not in peacetime to be arbitrarily pegged at artificial price levels, it was perhaps defensible for the monetary authorities to concentrate almost wholly on open market operations in the shortest-term government securities. Without entering into the merits of this position—and the problem is indeed anything but a simple one to be decided by emotional slogans—responsible economists realize that the new international situation requires some change in emphasis. Indeed it is encouraging to note that the Federal Reserve authorities have themselves already been experimenting with actions designed to adjust to the new situation. Still further actions may be desirable in order to help bring long-term interest rates down relative to short-term. It is long-term rates which are most decisive for investment spending; and it is short-term interest rates that are most decisive for foreign balances. This is not an area for hasty improvisation or doctrinaire reversal of policies; but it is one for pragmatic evolution of procedures and policies.

Nor is this merely a task for the Federal Reserve. The Treasury too must consider the wisdom of relying primarily on short-term issues in the period just ahead. Those in Congress who have thought that recession times are the best period in which to issue long-term debt at low interest rates will have to go through the same agonizing reappraisal of their view as a result of the new international situation.

The whole problem of debt management by the Treasury, as coordinated with the Federal Reserve in the interest of over-all stability, will require rethinking in these new times. No conflict of desires between the Executive and the Federal Reserve is to be involved, since both have the same interest in economic recovery and defense of the dollar.

(ii) Decisive actions to improve our international balance of payments position are desired for their own sake as well as to liberate domestic stabilization policies. This is not the place to describe the numerous programs that are needed in the international area. Fortunately there are some reasons to think that our net export position is an improving one and that the task is not an impossibly difficult one.

The primary need is to make sure that our productivity is improved so that our costs will remain competitive in international markets. But there are also certain measures that can alleviate the psychological drain on gold.

VI. "Second Line of Defense" Policies

14. *Two alternatives.* All the above has been premised upon a specific, and perhaps optimistic, forecast of how the economy is likely to behave in 1961. This first alternative could be called the "optimistic model" were it not for the fact that it turns out to involve unemployment that does not shrink much or any in 1961 below present levels of some 6 per cent. It seems nevertheless to agree most closely with the likeliest expectations revealed by a careful canvass of economic forecasters in business firms, universities, and public agencies.

Concretely, the optimistic model assumes that the Gross National Product will decline for at most one or two quarters. It assumes that the calendar year GNP will average out to between $510 and $515 billion, which represents an improvement in real GNP of about 2 per cent in real terms (after correction for price changes has been made). It assumes that by the end of the year the economy will be running some 3 per cent above the present rate. It assumes that even in the absence of any needed programs by the New Administration the current Budget will have lost its surplus and more likely will show some deficit. It assumes that our new jobs will be barely enough to provide work for the 1.2 million workers who are added to the labor force in 1961 and that unemployment remains a grave social problem.

Evidently such an outlook cannot be regarded as an optimistic one; and it is to improve upon this situation that the above programs were prescribed.

It is only wise, though, to be prepared for an even worse outlook. Suppose inventory decumulation continues longer than expected above; that consumers continue to save as large a percentage of their disposable incomes as they have recently been doing; that plant and equipment expenditures by business accelerate their downward slide; and that construction generally proves to be disappointing. What then?

In that case unemployment will rise toward and perhaps beyond the critical 7½ per cent level that marks the peak of the postwar era. In that case corporate profits will sink far below their present depressed levels, and a sagging stock market may add to the public's feeling of pessimism. In that case we shall certainly automatically incur a large deficit. While many hope and expect this more pessimistic model will not happen, it cannot be ruled out by careful students of economic history and present indications.

15. *A temporary tax cut.* If economic reports on business during the early months of the year begin to suggest that the second, more pessimistic, outlook is the more relevant one, then it will be the duty of public policy to take a more active, expansionary role. This is not the place to spell out the details of such a program. But certainly the following tax-cut measure will then deserve consideration.

A temporary reduction in tax rates on individual incomes can be a powerful weapon against recession. Congress should legislate, for example, a cut of 3 or 4 percentage points in the tax rate applicable to every income class, to take effect immediately under our withholding system in March or April and to continue until the end of the year.

In view of the great desirability of introducing greater flexibility into tax rates, it would be highly desirable for Congress to grant to the Executive the right to continue such a reduction for one or two six-month (or three-month) periods beyond that time (subject to the actions being set aside by Joint Resolution of Congress) with the clear understanding that the reduction will definitely expire by the end of 1962.

At this time it would be urgently important to make sure that any tax cut was clearly a temporary one. With the continued international uncertainty and with new public programs coming up in the years ahead, sound finance may require a maintenance of our present tax structure and any weakening of it in order to fight a recession might be tragic. Even if it should prove to be the case that growth makes reduction of tax rates possible in the long run, that should be a decision taken on its own merits and adopted along with a comprehensive reforming of our present tax structure. (Various tax devices to stimulate investment might also be part of a comprehensive program designed to eliminate loopholes, promote equity, and enhance incentives.)

VII. A Final Caution

16. *Direct attack on the wage-price spiral.* The above programs have been primarily concerned with fiscal and monetary policy. This is as it should be.

It is important, though, to realize that there are some problems that fiscal and monetary policy cannot themselves come to grips with.

Thus, if there is indeed a tendency for prices and wages to rise long before we reach high employment, neither monetary nor fiscal policy can be used to the degree necessary to promote desired growth.

What may then be needed are new approaches to the problem of productivity, wages and price formation. Will it not be possible to bring government influence to bear on this vital matter without invoking direct controls on wages and prices? Neither labor, nor management, nor the consumer can gain from an increase in price tags. Just as we pioneered in the 1920's in creating potent monetary mechanisms and in the 1930's in forging the tools of effective fiscal policy, so may it be necessary in the 1960's to meet head on the problem of a price creep. This is a challenge to mixed economies all over the free world, and is not to be met by government alone.

4: AREA REDEVELOPMENT

Introduction

The task force on area redevelopment was appointed by President John F. Kennedy to formulate a program of action to assist people in economically distressed areas.

These areas include (a) nearly 100 labor markets classified by the U.S. Department of Labor as areas of "substantial and persistent labor surplus," and (b) three to four hundred of the lowest-income rural-small urban areas plagued by underemployment.

A distressed area is typically a pocket of chronic unemployment which persists even during relatively prosperous times in the rest of the Nation. It is especially hard hit in times of recession. Currently, when the unemployment rate nationally is over 6 per cent, the distressed area rate is over 10 per cent, and in some instances as high as 20 per cent. General economic recovery can be expected to reduce the unemployment rate in distressed areas somewhat, but not enough to enable them to enjoy a fair share of the Nation's prosperity.

Changes in consumer demand, depletion of resources, changes in defense procurement or in location of defense facilities, decentralization of production, lack of industrial diversification, and technological change are the most important causes of depressed economic conditions in the labor surplus areas.

The use of gas and oil rather than coal for home heating and railroad power is an example of changed consumer demand. This shift in consumer preference, accompanied by mechanization of mining operations, resulted in serious unemployment in large areas of Indiana, Illinois, three regions of the Upper Great Lakes, Pennsylvania, Kentucky, West Virginia, and many other communities along the Appalachian Range.

Task Force: Senator Paul Douglas, chairman, Myer Feldman, William L. Batt, Jr., Earl T. Bester, Herbert J. Bingham, Harry A. Boswell, Jr., Thomas H. Bride, Jr., Dr. Clyde L. Colson, William R. Davlin, Wayne C. Fletcher, Dr. William Haber, Arthur L. Hamilton, Harry G. Hoffmann, John A. Kosinski, Dr. W. George Pinnell, Don B. Potter, John P. Robin, Burl A. Sawyers, Miles C. Stanley, Charles H. Stoddard, Laurence E. Tierney, Jr., John D. Whisman, Michael F. Widman, Jr.; Consultants: Senator Joseph S. Clark, Senator Jennings Randolph, Senator Robert C. Byrd, Representative Daniel Flood, Sol Barkin, Milton P. Semer.

Decreased consumer demand for wool textiles as a result of the development of synthetic fibers, as well as changes in plant location, have similarly left the textile towns of New England in a depressed condition.

The social impact of chronic unemployment is staggering. In September, 3.2 million persons obtained a distribution of Government surplus, amounting to a retail value of about only $9.36 per month per family of 4 persons. The number relying on surplus foods increases sharply in winter months. Along with the school lunch program, these surplus foods constitute the last line of resistance against malnutrition for hundreds of thousands of our fellow Americans. In West Virginia alone, in October, 281,000 people, out of a total population of 1.8 million, depended upon surplus food in order to sustain life.

There is wide bipartisan agreement that the distressed area problem cannot be resolved by private initiative alone. Government can lend a helping hand—local and State government as well as the Federal Government. It is also generally recognized that no one solution—no one plan or legislative enactment—can do the whole job for all distressed areas.

In the recommendations that follow, a diversity of programs is suggested. Some are urgent and demand immediate action, such as the relief of personal hardship, and the passage of an area redevelopment bill. Others refer to the priorities which should be assigned to the areas of chronic unemployment within existing or contemplated programs. Still others are recommendations which may be accepted or rejected, expanded or contracted, as experience is gained. Some are immediate and short-term. Others are long-range programs which cannot be carried out in a single year. Altogether, they serve as an arsenal from which specific weapons to combat the particular problems of a region or area may be selected.

I. Relief of Personal Hardship

1. *Food.* At present, flour, lard, dried eggs, dried milk, meal, and rice are on the surplus food distribution list. To improve the diet of needy persons in distressed areas, we recommend executive action to make additional surplus commodities available (such as butter, oatmeal, and peanut butter); to improve the distribution of surplus commodities with funds, personnel, storage space, and trucks; to assure that surplus commodities are made available regardless of State residence requirements; and to improve the management of the school lunch program so that it reaches every school in a distressed area.

We further recommend both executive and legislative action to permit the use of available funds to acquire foods temporarily not in surplus but necessary to provide a minimum balanced diet to those eligible for food grants; and both executive and legislative action to develop a food stamp plan, initially on a pilot basis, in the areas of greatest need.

2. *Unemployment compensation.* The current high national rate of unemployment has intensified the difficulties in the distressed areas. Unemployment insurance benefits have become the most significant first line of defense to eligible jobless wage earners. Our unemployment insurance legislation is in need of general improvement in the amount, duration, and financing of benefits. Pending such improvement, however, early action is necessary to meet the problems created by the exhaustion of unemployment insurance benefit rights for hundreds of thousands of wage earners.

To meet that problem, we recommend a temporary emergency unemployment insurance program along the general lines of the Temporary Unemployment Compensation Act of 1958. We urge, however, that the Federal funds advanced to the States should be in the form of grants rather than loans.

In addition, a Federal reinsurance program should be given high priority in the next Congress in order to protect States with a high proportion of distressed areas. Further increases in the taxes to finance unemployment compensation in those States will hinder efforts to attract new industry and will also discourage the growth of existing industry.

3. *General assistance.* The Federal system of grants-in-aid for public assistance does not provide any aid for the able-bodied, needy citizens and their families who have exhausted their unemployment compensation benefits. State programs for general assistance vary widely and most systems are inadequate to meet the needs. In 17 States, local funds are the only sources available to pay relief benefits to the employable needy, and the areas where the need is greatest often have the least economic resources from which to raise such funds.

We therefore recommend legislation to provide grants-in-aid to the States to help them finance adequate general assistance programs or, alternatively, an extension of the Federal aid-to-dependent-children program so that it will include children in need because their parents are unemployed.

4. *Emergency public work projects.* The question of whether a nationwide program of emergency public works projects should be

undertaken as an anti-recession measure is under consideration by another presidential task force. If such a program is authorized we believe that an appropriate portion of the available funds should be set aside for the distressed areas, and that among the authorized public works projects should be those for such purposes as local and regional access roads. These will be particularly helpful to distressed areas in overcoming their disadvantages in location and transportation. Distressed communities might also be relieved of some or all of any matching requirements, depending upon the extent of their resources. Also there should be projects which will enable these areas to develop their forest, water, and other resources.

If no national emergency public work programs are undertaken, then we recommend an emergency program of small public work projects limited to the distressed areas. The chronic low income in most of these areas has forced a chronic neglect of needed public works. Yet, without such improved public facilities, the private economy of these areas will probably never be successfully revived.

In the early 1930's, when we were struggling to overcome a national depression, we engaged in a great debate as to the relative desirability of public work projects as against direct relief. The decision was for public work, and for many reasons. The monuments of that decision—schools, improved forest and recreational areas, dams, roads, bridges—are now a part of our national wealth.

While we were then dealing with a national depression, an analogous situation exists when we are dealing—as we are now—with localized depressions. And for all of the reasons which contributed to a national decision for national public works to take people off the relief rolls and combat a national depression, we believe that a national decision should now be made for localized public works to take people off the relief rolls and combat localized depression.

Although eligibility standards for such aid must be drawn with great care, we believe that for the most distressed communities in the country there is no other adequate or self-respecting way to relieve long-standing hardship and begin the process of recovery.

II. Development of Long-term Job Opportunities

The proposals for improved programs for the distribution of surplus food, unemployment compensation, public assistance, and emergency public work projects — while imperative to alleviate immediate hardship—are not the ultimate answers to the problem of the distressed areas.

From the standpoint of long-term public policy, the need is for permanent jobs.

Jobs sustain the morale of individuals and communities. Jobs add to individual and national wealth. When a job is provided for a man on relief, a taxpayer is substituted for a recipient of public assistance expenditures.

And jobs, not relief, are what the people of the distressed areas want.

This task force assumes that prompt and energetic measures will be taken by the new administration to create conditions under which the Nation will return to an adequate rate of economic growth. We further assume that recommendations for countering the current recession and stimulating expansion of the national economy are beyond the scope of our assignment. But nothing, from the standpoint of our mission, is more important. Unless the national economy begins to grow at a rate fast enough to reduce substantially the current excessive national rate of unemployment, any special measures to benefit the distressed areas will be little more than palliatives.

The measures to insure adequate growth are varied. Some of them will operate quickly to provide job opportunities in the distressed areas; others will do so only over a longer period. But a many-sided program should be enacted now to channel national growth, in greater degree than in the past, into areas of high and persistent unemployment and underemployment. Even in a period of more rapid economic growth, supplementary measures will still be necessary to develop and rehabilitate these areas. Only then will these areas be able to share fully in the rising volume of national production, and, in turn, contribute to national growth.

1. *Area redevelopment legislation.* The most immediate need is for legislation which will encourage new industry to locate, and existing industry to expand, in industrial areas of chronic unemployment, and in underdeveloped rural and small urban areas of underemployment which require a better balance of industry and agriculture.

Bills specifically designed for this purpose passed the Congress in 1958 and in 1960. They were thoroughly considered in extensive hearings by congressional committees, and there is wide agreement as to the general approach. In view of the need for quick action, it is recommended that an area redevelopment bill be enacted promptly by the Congress, and sent to the President for his signature.

The area redevelopment bill should propose a coordinated effort by the Federal, State, and local governments and private enterprise to redevelop the economies of areas with chronic unemployment and underemployment.

Such a bill should contain four main features:

Technical assistance. Careful programming is essential to successful efforts for economic redevelopment. Technical assistance must be provided to local bodies to enable communities and areas to plan intelligently their long-term economic development, explore fully the most constructive lines for their expansion, and create new locational advantages within their communities to attract private and public enterprise. Financial provisions should be contained within the legislation to enable the Administrator to assist these communities in programming their development course.

Loans for private projects. The construction of industrial and commercial buildings, including tourist facilities, at attractive financial terms is frequently essential to the economic redevelopment of distressed areas and the creation of jobs. The evidence is conclusive that conventional lending facilities in distressed areas cannot provide fully for the long-term credit needed for such construction. The area redevelopment bill, therefore, should provide for loans that will attract business firms to these areas. Because the Federal Government should not subsidize these loans, the interest rate should therefore be fixed somewhat higher than the Federal Government pays on loans of comparable maturities. The bill should require that at least 35 per cent of the capital investment come from non-Federal sources.

The purpose of financing these new projects is to assist in the creation of new enterprises rather than in the relocation of established firms.

Loans and grants for public facilities. Modernized public facilities are often prerequisites to the establishment or expansion of industrial or commercial plants or facilities. Some communities are unable to support the needed public facilities because of limited financial resources resulting from the deterioration of the tax base or chronic low income.

A loan program is needed to realize these facilities in such communities. In extreme cases it will be necessary to provide grants to enable communities to provide the facilities, such as access roads, industrial water, industrial parks, and public utilities where lacking, to make them attractive for industrial or commercial facilities. In most cases it is anticipated that grants will be related to the ability of the community and the State to contribute to such ventures.

Training, Retraining, and Subsistence. It is also essential for a successful redevelopment program that the Federal Government, in cooperation with State, local, and private organizations expand the facilities and opportunities for training and retraining the labor force in the distressed areas in the new skills required in industry and commerce.

To make it financially possible for workers to undertake the training and retraining, those who are not entitled to or have exhausted their unemployment insurance should be paid subsistence payments during the period of training and retraining.

Secondary market for industrial mortgages. Many communities which have suffered heavy unemployment over a long period have invested large sums, including funds raised by popular subscription through community development organizations, in long-term industrial mortgages. But these communities, some of which pioneered in self-help operations, now find their available risk capital tied up in these mortgages, and are running out of financial resources. In order to free their funds for new investment in enterprises which will create the required new jobs, the Area Redevelopment Administrator should study the feasibility of allowing financial institutions in distressed areas, especially community development groups, to rediscount their industrial mortgages with some agency of the Federal Government. This could follow the general pattern established for the purchase of real estate mortgages by the Federal National Mortgage Association.

Loan Insurance. The Administrator should also study the desirability of establishing a program of loan insurance to supplement the direct loan program contemplated in the area redevelopment program.

2. *Federal procurement.* We are deeply concerned that only about 1 per cent of the value of all military prime contract awards is assigned to areas of substantial labor surplus as a result of any action by the military departments to assist these areas.

(a) We recommend that there be established at the requirements planning levels of defense and defense-related agencies positions to be filled by highly qualified technicians, employed by a different agency of the Federal Government, with responsibility to recommend ways and means to most effectively utilize production and manpower capabilities in areas of substantial labor surplus, including small businesses, in these areas.

We recommend that the President direct procurement agencies to require prime contractors to submit in their proposed bids detailed information regarding the maximum use of manpower and facilities located in substantial and persistent labor surplus areas. The procurement agencies should then require successful bidders to carry out such plans.

(b) It should be the policy of the Federal Government to encourage firms in distressed areas to participate fully in Government procurement. We recommend that the President direct Federal procurement agencies to make maximum use of competitive bids and set-asides. We also recommend that procurement agencies energetically implement the provisions of Defense Manpower Order No. 4 by assuring that firms in distressed areas participate to the maximum extent in Government procurement activities.

(c) If a general Government policy is adopted looking toward the additional dispersal of plants for defense production and defense related installations, we believe that labor surplus areas should be given preferred consideration in the choosing of these new sites. The same principle should apply with respect to the dispersal, relocation, or new location of non-defense agencies and facilities of the Federal Government.

(d) In view of evidence submitted to the Task Force that some distressed areas have been deprived of some of their markets when other more expensive fuels have been offered to Government-owned installations, we recommend that an Executive order be issued which will require that all Government-owned installations now in existence, or which may be constructed, should use that fuel which is most economical on the basis of an accurate, realistic, and impartial cost survey.

3. *The development of human resources.* The long-continued low income levels in some of the Nation's distressed and underdeveloped regions have also resulted in a relative underdevelopment of human talent. Local financial resources have not been sufficient to provide educational opportunities which are equal to those of other areas, and a large proportion of the more highly educated individuals have left their home communities for the more prosperous sections of the country. This migration has in turn handicapped these areas in their efforts to attain a healthy role of economic growth.

To reverse this trend requires outside help.

Raising of educational standards. The educational lag in these regions cannot be overcome without Federal aid. It is the assumption of this task force that Federal aid on a nationwide basis will be instituted during the coming year. We recommend that such a program should embody an equalization formula to assure additional assistance to the poorer areas. Once such a program is enacted, we recommend that the President instruct the Secretary of Health, Education, and Welfare to determine what further legislation may be needed to enable these areas to provide educational opportunities equal to those offered citizens who live elsewhere, and to deal in the immediate future with the special education and training problems which currently limit the opportunities of young people in these areas.

Training, retraining, and placement. Studies have shown that even in areas of high unemployment and even in the midst of recessions there are jobs for those with the right skills. Moreover, the possession of a skill which is in demand can enable an unemployed person to leave the area to find employment elsewhere.

Pending new legislative authority, a supplemental appropriation should be sought under the Vocational Act of 1946 earmarked for this specific purpose in order to permit a beginning to be made in the fiscal year 1961.

The Secretary of Health, Education, and Welfare and the Secretary of Labor should investigate the feasibility of providing funds to defray the cost of transportation to jobless workers while undergoing training.

Entering upon a retraining program should moreover not disqualify for unemployment compensation a person who is otherwise eligible.

In addition, the Secretary of Labor should make a special study to see how the functions of the employment service may be improved, so that available workers can be more effectively matched with available jobs.

Services to persons with special employment problems. A person looking for work may have a special disadvantage if he is too old or too young, if he is unskilled or has the wrong skill, if he has a physical handicap, or if he is colored. While the problems of "hard to place" persons are national in scope, they are always more severe in areas of heavy unemployment.

The Employment Service has a smaller staff today than 13 years ago (10,460 compared to 12,124). We recommend placing additional specially trained vocational counselors in key employment offices in redevelopment areas to serve workers who have special employment problems. We also recommend sending task forces of experts in counseling, guidance, and job development into a community whenever a major unemployment crisis such as a mine or plant shutdown either occurs or threatens to occur.

To ease the burden of unemployment on the older workers, we recommend the amendment of the Social Security Act to permit retirement of male workers at age 62 with correspondingly reduced annuities.

We further recommend that the President establish a Committee on Special Problems of the Labor Force, and assign its responsibility

for a program of educational and community planning and action to
break down arbitrary barriers to the employment of all the groups of
disadvantaged workers.

Manpower studies. We believe that responsibility should be clearly
placed upon an existing or new unit in the Executive Office of the
President to provide the leadership for and the coordination of the
activities of the Federal Government in the entire area of manpower
and the development of human resources.

4. *The development of physical resources and use of other special
inducements.* Many of the Nation's distressed communities are located
in underdeveloped regions with a rich natural resource potential. Yet,
because of disadvantages of transportation, location, and topography,
often mounting to inaccessibility, these resources have not been developed as rapidly as those of other areas. Lack of development has resulted in relatively low income, which, in turn, has resulted in a
deficiency of capital. To reverse this downward spiral requires outside
capital. In some cases the resource, such as a forest, has been depleted
and is no longer an adequate source of employment in the production
of timber, water development, and outdoor recreational facilities.

As resources are rehabilitated income and capital will be generated
locally, providing the base of needed economic growth.

The emergency public work programs, the area redevelopment legislation, and other programs and actions proposed in this report should
be administered with a view to their maximum contribution to the
long-term development of the natural resources of the distressed areas.
In addition, Federal assistance on a long-term basis is needed in several
specific resource categories:

Highways. The curtailment of the Federal-aid highway program
throughout the Nation by imposition of contract controls has had a
particularly injurious effect on States containing distressed areas, because these are the States which, because of relatively low income,
have lagged in highway construction. We recommend that the President take executive action to terminate the restrictions which have
prevented the States from making use of the full amount of Federal-
aid highway funds legally available to them.

We recommend further that the President urge the several States,
wherever feasible within the framework of prescribed criteria, to give
priority to highway improvement projects located in or near economically distressed areas.

Special emphasis should be given to bringing chronically distressed
areas into the mainstream of economic life through feeder road con-

struction where isolation of large numbers of people prevents modern economic development.

The criteria for highway routing and capacity should take into account how economic growth can be stimulated, particularly in areas which have lagged in growth.

Forests. As part of the program for emergency public works, a supplemental appropriation should be made to the Forest Service for the current fiscal year to permit timber-stand improvement, reforestation, trail and road construction, watershed improvement, erosion control, and development of recreation facilities in national forests in or adjacent to distressed areas.

For a longer range program, we recommend that the President direct the Secretary of Agriculture to present to the Congress during 1961 a plan for forest development in distressed areas, to include restoration of productivity and income-producing capability of the small private forest lands and strip-mined forest areas.

In addition to accelerating the conservation work on the national forests at once, their long-range plans should be adjusted and accelerated in a way that will give emphasis to the work needed in distressed areas over the next several years. There should also be fully utilized the authority to create new national forests where this solution is indicated.

Parks. Similarly, a supplemental appropriation should be made to the National Park Service for Mission 66 projects in areas of economic distress with special emphasis upon facilities which will encourage the tourist industry.

To help promote the tourist industry in distressed areas, special authorization and appropriation should be provided to assist States to develop recreational facilities, such as roadside parks and campsites. The program would be administered by the National Park Service in cooperation with the States.

Agricultural conservation. As part of the emergency program, a supplemental appropriation should be made for the current fiscal year to the Soil Conservation Service for a land conservation work program to be administered through local soil conservation districts. The work to be stressed would include reforestation on farms and strip mine spoil areas, stream bank stabilization and erosion control, and small water control structures.

As a long-term measure, funds in the agricultural conservation program should be earmarked for permanent conservation practices providing maximum local employment in distressed areas, such as forestry on private land held by low-income landlords, with up to 100 per cent of the cost to be borne by the Federal Government. Manpower would be obtained from local unemployed personnel, and the work to be stressed should be timber stand improvement and erosion control.

Fuels and minerals. The coal and fossil fuel rich areas need basic and applied research to provide new uses to maintain existing uses and to promote stability of employment.

We recommend an additional appropriation for the new Office of Coal Research and the intensification of cooperative studies with State and private groups.

In some areas higher quality minerals have been exhausted while elsewhere they are being neglected because methods have not been developed economically to extract and process certain low quality ores, or sufficient economic uses have not yet been discovered for other minerals. We propose, therefore, that the minerals research program of the Bureau of Mines be expanded.

We recommend development of a national fuels policy. The lack of a national fuels policy is an underlying reason for some of the existing conditions of distress in the coal producing regions and in some independent oil producing communities. A national fuels policy would help alleviate prevalent distress, would help improve the economic health of these industries, and would be beneficial to the Nation's security.

Other public works. A supplemental appropriation should be made to initiate construction of authorized projects for clear streams, navigation and flood control, pollution abatement, sealing of abandoned mines, public buildings, and other public works projects in or near areas of economic distress.

The agencies should be instructed to initiate or accelerate planning on new projects which provide opportunities for economic development in distressed areas, and to submit for Presidential approval projects on which planning is complete and which are ready for authorization.

The U.S. Army Engineers should be urged to take a new look in labor surplus areas at water resource projects previously classed as inactive so as to determine the possibility of their being placed again in the active category, and proper consideration should be given to all factors, including even flow and employment benefits in the selection of projects for authorization.

Youth Conservation Corps. We recommend enactment of a bill to create a Youth Conservation Corps as provided by S.812, passed by the Senate in 1959. Such a corps would provide manpower to expedite some of the kinds of projects of the type discussed earlier for National and State forests and parks while drawing enrollees locally to the greatest extent feasible and giving priority to locally experienced men as supervisors.

Consideration of special tax amortization. As additional encouragement to private industry to locate branch plants in chronic and persistent labor surplus areas and to expand existing enterprises in these areas, consideration should be given to the question of whether special tax amortization providing for accelerated writeoffs of plant and equipment would help to encourage industries to locate or expand production facilities in such areas.

5. *Special regional development problems.* We believe that in some regions of the country, where economic problems are particularly deep-seated and severe, the resource development activities described above need to be coordinated into broad regional developmental programs.

A region where such an approach is appropriate may be defined as one which although it may contain islands of prosperity, suffers retarded economic growth in the region as a whole, has a level of income well below those of surrounding regions, and experiences a general underutilization of its labor force.

One such region is easy to identify—the Appalachian area which extends from New York to Alabama and contains portions of 11 States. The economy of the region suffers from the decline of the coal industry, disadvantages of topography, transportation, and highway deficiencies, and isolation from major population centers.

Other regions with special problems include the textile region of New England and upper New York; the region of declining timber and iron ore production of the upper Great Lakes States; certain underdeveloped rural and small-town areas of the South, Southwest, and Far West; and the coal region of southern Illinois and Indiana.

We urge a program of regional development commissions to attack the special problems of each region and to propose means for formulating and carrying out comprehensive development programs.

As an immediate step, we recommend that the President appoint such a commission for at least one of these major areas. Both because of its size and the severity of its problems, we believe that such a commission might well be set up first for the Appalachian region. This in turn could serve as a possible pilot project for similar efforts in other regions.

6. *The prevention of distressed areas.* Our recommendations thus

far have related to the alleviation of distress and economic revival within areas now classified as distressed.

Of perhaps equal importance, though infinitely more difficult, is the development of an early warning system to detect the beginning of trends which lead to localized depressions and the development of measures for the correction of such trends before the problem becomes acute.

It is now apparent that the automation of particular industries, such as the steel industry, may result in a new group of distressed areas.

We therefore recommend that the President give consideration, through whatever agency he deems appropriate, to the problem of structural changes in the economy which produce unemployment, with particular emphasis on automation and with the job of devising such an early warning system together with remedial measures.

5: SOCIAL WELFARE FRONTIERS

Introduction

The task force on health and social security was appointed by President-elect Kennedy to review from among the most pressing and significant health and welfare proposals those which should have priority in the initial phase of the new Administration.

The recommendations of the task force consist of the following proposals:

A. *Medical and Health Programs*

1: Medical Care for the Aged and Other Social Security Beneficiaries. 2: Medical Education and Medical Manpower. 3: Medical Research. 4: Medical Care Facilities. 5: Establishment of a National Academy of Health. 6: Creation of a National Institute of Child Health.

B. *Services For Families, Children and Older Persons*

7: Assistance to Children of an Unemployed Parent. 8: Preparation of a Family and Child Welfare Services Plan. 9: Strengthening and Streamlining Administrative Organization. 10: (not for release). 11: (not for release). 12: (not for release).

The task force has had available to it the public recommendations of various groups, and a substantial body of data, including the information and conclusions in the following official reports which have been of inestimable value to it in making its recommendations:

Federal Support of Medical Research: Report of the Committee of Consultants on Medical Research to the Senate Committee on Appropriations (The Jones Report), 1960.

Physicians for a Growing America: Report of the Surgeon General's Consultant Group on Medical Education (The Bane Report), 1959.

The Advancement of Medical Research and Education Through the

Task force: Wilbur J. Cohen, chairman, Dean A. Clark, James Dixon, Herman M. Somers, Robert E. Cooke, Joshua Lederberg, Elizabeth Wickenden.

Department of Health, Education and Welfare (The Bayne-Jones Report), 1958.

Hospitalization Insurance for OASDI Beneficiaries: Report Submitted to the Committee on Ways and Means by the Secretary of Health, Education, and Welfare (The Flemming Report), 1959.

Report of the Advisory Council on Public Assistance (The Mitchell Report), 1906.

Report of the Advisory Council on Child Welfare Services (The Kidneigh Report), 1959.

The Condition of American Nursing Homes, A Study by the Subcommittee on Problems of the Aged and Aging of the Senate Committee on Labor and Public Welfare (The McNamara Committee), 1960.

Report of the Special Committee on Unemployment Problems, 86th Congress, 2nd Session, Report No. 1206 (The Eugene McCarthy Committee), 1960.

The task force urges the favorable consideration of the proposals discussed in this report.

An adequate standard of health and welfare for all of the American people requires the leadership and support of the Federal government.

The American people have recognized and accepted the responsibility of the Federal Government to help improve health and welfare services. This principle requires effective implementation in 1961.

The Task Force has confined itself to the most immediate necessities for Federal action and does not present its recommendations as a complete program for health and welfare. We have been deeply conscious of the need for selectivity in the light of the cost of such proposals in relation to the other imperative and immediate fiscal and administrative demands upon the Federal government. We have also been concerned about the most effective and practical methods of meeting these costs and are proposing fiscally sound methods to achieve the desired objectives. Our proposals place a major reliance on the self-financing methods of contributory social insurance and repayable loans supplemented only where clearly necessary by funds from the general revenues.

A. Medical and Health Programs

The United States can be proud of its remarkable and continually improving health and medical care personnel, facilities and programs.

Yet, in our country there are still significant medical care needs
which can and should be met and which can only be met if the
Federal government takes a more vigorous role in the financing,
organization and stimulation of health and medical care.

1. MEDICAL CARE FOR THE AGED AND OTHER SOCIAL SECURITY BENE-
    FICIARIES

The only sound and practical way of meeting the health needs of
most older people is through the contributory social security system.
This system permits people to contribute during their working years
to the relatively heavy costs of medical care in their later years.
Full freedom in the choice of qualified physicians and medical facilities
would be assured. The proposal uses the tried and tested insurance
method payment for hospital and medical care with which millions
of Americans of working age are familiar through Blue Cross and
other private insurance. The same general considerations apply to
widows, surviving children, and permanently disabled persons who
are receiving social security payments.

Scope of Medical Care Benefits. Hospital and related institutional
costs place such an impossibly heavy financial burden on these groups
of people that these costs should receive the major emphasis in any
program. Moreover, the hospital is increasingly becoming the center
of health activities in the community—as it should be. But at the
same time the plan should include incentives to use appropriate alternative personnel and facilities of a less costly and non-institutional
character.

The essential benefits in any such program at this time should
include: (1) inpatient hospital service; (2) out-patient hospital diagnostic services, (3) skilled nursing home services, (4) home health
services, such as visiting nurse services.

The inpatient and out-patient hospital services would be effective
approximately one year after enactment of the legislation. To give
time to make necessary arrangements skilled nursing services and
home health services would be available two years after enactment.
By including in the legislation provisions which would give an individual two units of skilled nursing home service for one day of hospital
service and adequate home health services there would be an incentive to use these out-of-hospital services.

There are those who contend that there are not sufficient personnel
and facilities to make it feasible to put this program into effect at

this time. Certainly, incentives should be created for the establishment of additional personnel and facilities as recommended subsequently in this report. But this should not be a reason for delay in
instituting an insurance program. One of the most important ways in
which personnel and facilities are stimulated and more equitably distributed is by providing a mechanism for paying for such services.
Assurance of continued financial support for service is one of the
key elements in the development of personnel and facilities.

Administration of Medical Care Program. The legislation would
clearly provide that:

(1) In no way will any of its provisions socialize medical care;

(2) Free choice of physician, hospital, and nursing home are assured to every individual by law;

(3) There would be no supervision or control over the practice of
medicine;

(4) Providers of service would be paid on the basis of reasonable
cost as may be mutually agreed to by the provider of service and the
Secretary of Health, Education, and Welfare and any agreement could
be terminated upon notice by either party;

(5) Providers of service could designate an agent to negotiate arrangements with the Federal government;

(6) A national advisory council would be established including outstanding persons in the hospital and health fields. The Council would
be consulted in the development of policy and regulations in the
administration of the program;

(7) General definitions for participating hospitals, skilled nursing
homes, and agencies providing home health services would be indicated
in the statute. The Secretary should be authorized to use appropriate
State agencies in determining whether a particular hospital, skilled
nursing home or home health agency meets the definition for participation.

Financing of the Medical Care Program. The cost of the medical
care benefits should be fully financed by contributions to the insurance
system. The costs of various alternatives are shown in Table 1.

A plan which involved initial contributions of about 0.5 per cent
of taxable payrolls (one-quarter per cent each on employers and
employees) during the first five to ten years and then stepped up
contributions to about 0.8 per cent (0.14% on each party) would permit the development of a reasonably adequate benefit program consistent with a consideration of the financial effect of the new contributions on the contributors and the economy.

ESTIMATES OF EARLY YEAR[1] AND LEVEL PREMIUM COST[2] FOR THE
ANDERSON KENNEDY AMENDMENT OF 1960 AND
VARIOUS SUGGESTED MODIFICATIONS
as a Per cent of Taxable Payrolls

Specifications of Medical Insurance Plan	Early Year Costs with taxable earnings base of:		Level Premium Costs with taxable earnings base of:	
	$4800	$7200	$4800	$7200
A. Anderson-Kennedy Amendment[3]	0.39	0.34	0.58	0.53
B. Anderson-Kennedy Amendment with elimination of $75 deductible	0.47	0.41	0.72	0.65
C. Anderson-Kennedy Amendment in (A) plus eligibility at age 65/62	0.53	0.46	0.73	0.66
D. Anderson-Kennedy Amendment in (A) plus eligibility at age 65/62 and elimination of $75 deductible	0.64	0.56	0.91	0.83
E. Anderson-Kennedy Amendment in (C) plus survivors and disabled beneficiaries	0.57	0.50	0.77	0.70
F. Anderson-Kennedy Amendment in (D) plus survivors and disabled beneficiaries	0.69	0.61	0.96	0.88

Source: Chief Actuary, Social Security Administration, January 5, 1961. The estimates differ slightly from those used in mid-1960 due in part to the 1960 changes in the OASDI program and some revisions in the assumptions.

[1] Early year costs are defined as the costs for the year 1962 assuming all features of the program are fully operative for the entire year.

[2] Level premium cost is the average cost for the long-run.

[3] As offered in the Senate, August 1960. The admendment included insured persons age 68 and over.

The contributory insurance system should be authorized to provide funds for:

(1) Community demonstration projects relating to the development of personnel and facilities to meet the health needs of individuals under the program;

(2) Community projects on the means to increase the adequacy of personnel and facilities;

(3) Consultative services to the States looking toward methods for helping develop adequate facilities within each State, and bringing their services and their facilities up to needed levels of performance.

The Secretary should make recommendations to the President and the Congress to encourage the development of economical and appropriate forms of health care which are a constructive alternative to hospitalization.

Coverage of aged not insured under social security. Many of the noninsured aged are already protected under other existing programs. Thus, under recently enacted provisions of law Federal civil service annuitants will soon have medical care protection. Veterans who are eligible for veterans' pension or compensation are entitled to hospitalization. Accompanying legislation can be enacted by Congress so that railroad retirement annuitants will have benefits no less favorable than social security beneficiaries. The small remaining group can be taken care of by the States under the new program of medical assistance to the aged. Enactment of the medical insurance plan will relieve the States of a substantial long-run cost involving probably more than $300 million annually. If experience demonstrates that the existing financial or other plan provisions of the Federal medical assistance legislation are not adequate to meet this residual need, then further Federal legislation can and should be enacted as the need is demonstrated.

*   *   *

The benefit, financing, administrative and other implications and alternatives in this program have been discussed with the Commissioner of Social Security. The details of a sound and workable plan consistent with the above program are in the process of completion by the Commissioner for the consideration and appropriate action of the incoming Secretary of Health, Education, and Welfare.

2. MEDICAL EDUCATION AND MEDICAL MANPOWER

In order to achieve the Administration's objective with respect to medical care for the aged as well as the health of the population as a whole, it is essential that the Federal government take prompt action to increase the supply of medical and other health personnel including physicians, dentists, nurses, public health personnel, and social workers. It is a matter of national concern that according to the Bane report to the Surgeon General 40 per cent of all medical students come from the 8 per cent of the families with the highest incomes.

A program for medical education and medical manpower should consist of the following inter-dependent components which are listed in the order of urgency:

1. Federal support for maintenance and expansion of educational activities in the health field consisting of:

a. A program for the basic support of operating costs to maintain these institutions.

b. A program which would give institutions an incentive to expand the training of personnel.

This part of the program would involve Federal expenditures of approximately $10 to $20 million in the first year.

2. Federal aid for the construction of new educational facilities and renovation and expansion of existing facilities for the purpose of increasing the numbers of persons being trained in these fields. This would consist of:

a. Planning grants to institutions to achieve these objectives ($400,000).

b. Alteration of existing facilities for expansion ($25,000,000 for first year).

c. New construction of facilities including expansion of existing schools and establishment of new ones. Within this category, with regard to physician training, priority should be given to expansion of existing schools and the establishment of new two year schools. (The Federal commitment would be about $25,000,000 for the first year but actual expenditures would be substantially less.)

3. Federal grants to institutions for scholarships and fellowships for students. This would involve Federal expenditures of about $10 to $20 million for the first year. These educational grants should be available to students so they could attend a medical school without regard to residence or other arbitrary restrictions not related to the ability of the applicant.

The program recommended by the Task Force would involve Federal funds of about $70 to $90 million in the first year. The cost will increase to about $270 million by the fourth year and is likely to remain at approximately that level. This is only about one half of the existing research grant program of the National Institutes of Health. The expenditure of these sums is essential for national growth and effective performance.

3. MEDICAL RESEARCH

The needs for medical research and research education have been admirably documented in the report to the Senate Committee on Appropriations of the Committee of Consultants on Medical Research under the chairmanship of Boisfeuillet Jones. The principles and recommendations in the Jones report would well serve as a longer-run guide to policy and appropriations in this field.

Federal support of the direct costs of medical research should be continued at approximately its present level for the next fiscal year. However, the educational and research activities of institutions receiving grants from the National Institutes of Health are handicapped at the present time by the limitation in the appropriation act on indirect costs. This limitation now at 15 per cent of the direct cost does not cover the actual indirect expenses. This acts as a deterrent to new research and reduces the available institutional funds for educational purposes. The Federal government as it does in other grants for research, should realistically meet the total costs of the research for which it makes grants through the National Institutes of Health. The first year cost would be about $20 million additional if this policy were applied to initial and renewed research grants only. The longer-run cost of this policy would be about $50 million annually.

4. Medical Care Facilities

The proposed medical care for the aged program will require additional facilities to be constructed over a period of time. The Hill-Burton hospital construction program has resulted in a significant increase in hospital beds, especially in small communities. There still remains, however, a substantial need for the construction and renovation of kinds of facilities required for the care of the older age group, especially in urban areas.

The first emphasis should be given to the following components in a program for facilities expansion:

a. An increase in existing Federal grants under the Hill-Burton Act for facilities for long-term care including public and non-profit skilled nursing home and other chronic disease facilities ($10 million annual increase).

b. Long-term low-interest Federal loans for construction, renovation and expansion of non-profit hospitals and nursing homes according to approved State plans. ($100 million annually). A combination of loans and grants should be permitted.

c. Long-term low-interest Federal loans for construction, renovation or expansion of facilities for medical group practice and group practice agencies or organizations (direct to the groups or agencies concerned, without the intervention of States). ($5 million annually).

An exploration should be made of possible ways in which existing legislation relating to loans to proprietary skilled nursing homes under the Small Business Administration could be amended to increase the proportion of cost guaranteed up to 95 per cent provided the homes met the standards of construction and continued operation prescribed by the U.S. Public Health Service as a part of a State plan.

The Secretary and the Surgeon General should take the leadership and initiative within existing legislation to encourage the development of outpatient diagnostic and treatment programs. Expansion of services in this setting will be of great importance to the successful operation of the medical care program for the aged.

5. ESTABLISHMENT OF A NATIONAL ACADEMY OF HEALTH

The President should take the necessary steps to arrange for the establishment of a National Academy of Health comparable to the National Academy of Sciences. The purpose of such a non-governmental, independent Academy would be two-fold:

a. To recognize and honor the significant achievements of leaders in health research, teaching, care and administration, and

b. To insure a continuing body of recognized integrity, responsibility of purpose, and breadth of competence for advice to the Government and the public on questions affecting health.

6. CREATION OF A NATIONAL INSTITUTE OF CHILD HEALTH

As an important new step in a broader program for the improvement in family and child health and welfare services, the Surgeon General, with the approval of the Secretary, should, by administrative action establish a National Institute of Child Health within the National Institutes of Health. Such action would recognize the Administration's concern not only with the welfare of the aged, but with its children and youth.

The establishment of the National Institute of Child Health would not require additional federal expenditures for research for the fiscal year 1962. An allocation from existing funds should be made for an initial administrative organization. Subsequent allocations of funds would be included within the budget of the National Institutes of Health.

The high incidence of mental disease, the terrifying problems of juvenile delinquency, the burden on family and community resources for the care of the mentally retarded, all attest to the need for a concentrated attack on problems of the development of the child. Research into the physical, intellectual and emotional growth of the child is at present severely handicapped by the absence of a central focus for research that exists in other fields such as heart disease and cancer. Within this Institute will be concentrated research workers in the fields of genetics, obstetrics, psychology and pediatrics as well as basic scientists who will channel their efforts into the study of the normal processes of human maturation from conception through adolescence.

Such a research program will have a profound impact on the medical care and practice in this nation by emphasizing the care of the whole individual rather than the fragmentation of the patient into particular diseases. The research grants from this Institute will stimulate programs necessary to ascertain those genetic and environmental factors that lead to the development of a physically and mentally healthy adult. Such an Institute should help bring to each child of this nation — normal, gifted, or retarded — complete fulfillment of his true potential.

B. *Services to Families, Children, and Older Persons*

A nation's strength lies in the well-being of its people: families, children, and older persons. Welfare services support this well-being in times of stress and constitute, therefore, an essential part of any effective social security program. It seems appropriate after twenty-five years that the welfare grant-in-aid provisions of the Social Security Act, especially those involving families and children, be re-examined to determine how they can be made more adequate to meet current social and economic needs. The following specific recommendations in this section are made with this objective in mind.

7. ASSISTANCE TO CHILDREN OF AN UNEMPLOYED PARENT

In order to meet the growing emergency needs of families affected by unemployment a temporary provision (until June 30, 1962) should be added to Title IV of the Social Security Act which would authorize the inclusion of children in need because of the unemployment of a parent among those eligible for Aid to Dependent Children. The provision would be temporary pending the development of the plan proposed in recommendations 8 and 12.

8. PREPARATION OF A FAMILY AND CHILD WELFARE SERVICES PLAN

The Secretary of Health, Education, and Welfare should be requested to develop for submission to the President and Congress, prior to the expiration of the temporary amendment to aid to dependent children, a Family and Child Welfare Services plan which would bring together in one program the resources of Federal aid to the States under the Social Security Act for assistance and social services to needy families and children and community social services in such areas as juvenile delinquency prevention, services to the aging, and other related programs designed to strengthen community life. This would not affect Titles I and X of the Social Security Act relating to the aged and the blind, respectively.

9. STENGTHENING ADMINISTRATIVE ORGANIZATION

The strengthening of services to families, children, and older persons also could be advanced through administrative action looking to a more effective organization within the Department of Health, Education, and Welfare. The following suggestions should be explored.

a. Elevation of the Children's Bureau from its present location within the Social Security Administration to the Secretary's office to serve its original purpose as a staff agency concerned with all the problems of child life and the promotion of new programs to meet them rather than with program operation.

b. Designation of the Special Staff on Aging as an Office of Aging to advise and assist the Secretary in a similar role with respect to the problems of older persons. This office would not carry any administrative functions.

c. Creation of an Institute of Family and Child Welfare Research associated with the Social Security Administration to combine the present research and demonstration functions enacted in 1956 and now vested in the Social Security Administration, including those of the Children's Bureau in the child welfare field.

d. Transfer of the administration of the Maternal and Child Health and Crippled Children grant programs to the Public Health Service.

e. Transfer of the administration of the Child Welfare Services program to the Social Security Commissioner pending the development of the combined Family and Child Welfare Services plan recommended in the Task Force Report.

This plan would combine the advantages of assuring spokesmen for

the needs of children and older persons at the top level of policy decision in the Deartment of Health, Education, and Welfare with those
implicit in a comprehensive approach to research, health, and welfare
services at the operational level. (See also related recommendations
6 and 12).

It appears that no new legislation would be required to carry out
these administrative suggestions since all program responsibilities are
now vested in the Secretary of Health, Education, and Welfare and he
is empowered to carry them out as he sees fit.

6: EDUCATIONAL FRONTIERS

I. FEDERAL SUPPORT FOR THE PUBLIC SCHOOL SYSTEM

The national interest demands a first-rate system of schools and that every child have full opportunity to benefit from that system. Present standards and facilities must be improved. Millions of children, particularly in certain rural areas and in the great cities, are deprived of an opportunity to develop talents that are needed both for society and for their own lives. The Task Force Committee concludes that first priority should be given to a vigorous program to lift the schools to a new level of excellence.

State and local governments alone cannot provide the funds needed. Federal support is required. The Task Force Committee recommends that action be taken in three closely related areas: a general program of support for all public schools to reach the new level; a special program for States in economic distress in providing for schools; and a special program for city schools.

(1) The Task Force Committee recommends that the President support legislation to provide $30 per annum per pupil, based on average daily attendance in public schools. The funds should be sent to the States for transmission to local boards of education on the basis of average daily attendance in their public schools. The boards of education should be authorized to use the funds for construction, salaries, or other purposes related to the improvement of education. The program should require State and local governments to maintain or increase their support of education. The annual cost is estimated at $1.2 billion.

(2) The Task Force Committee recommends that the President support legislation designed to provide $20 per child for States with personal income per student in average daily attendance in public schools that is below 70 per cent of the national average. The legislation should include provision to assure maintenance of State and local effort, and funds should be available for construction, salaries, or other

Task force: Frederick Hovde, President of Purdue University, chairman; Russell Thackrey, Executive Secretary of the Land Grant Colleges Association; Benjamin Willis, Superintendent of Schools, Chicago; Alvin Eurich, Vice President of the Ford Foundation; John Gardner, President of the Carnegie Corporation.

purposes related to the improvement of education in the public schools, as the State may determine. It is estimated that roughly one-quarter of the States might benefit from this legislation (mostly in the South), that approximately 7 million children would be helped toward full educational opportunity, and that the annual cost would be $140 million.

(3) The Task Force Committee recommends that the President support legislation designed to provide an amount equivalent to $20 per child in average daily attendance in the public schools of the great cities (over 300,000 population) which are facing unique and grave educational problems. The legislation should authorize the U.S. Commissioner of Education to make grants to such cities based upon plans proposed by their boards of education or by boards together with other boards of education within their area, for support of research and experimental programs in the special problems of these urban schools, for the planning and construction of facilities, for the acquisition of land sites, for the improvement of programs of community service by the schools, and for the strengthening of guidance and job placement programs for pupils over 16 years of age. Eligibility for such grants should be based on a formula which includes density of population, nature of housing, and per cent of students finishing high school. Provisions to assure maintenance of local effort should be included, as well as coordination with Federal and local housing agencies. It is estimated that the education of approximately 6 million children can be improved at a cost of $120 million annually.

II. Federal Support Program for Housing and Academic Facilities for the Colleges and Universities

(1) Grant and loan program for academic facilities. Although college and university enrollments are now at an all-time high, the period of greatest increase in enrollments is immediately ahead. In order to give urgently needed aid to colleges and universities (including junior colleges) to accommodate a million new students in the next 5 years, Congress should be urged to enact legislation providing for a combined program of loans and grants of at least $500 million for the first year, of which $350 million (70 per cent) should be for matching grants and $150 million (30 per cent) should be for loans on the same basis as the college housing loan program. In succeeding years this program will require increasing sums annually to meet the evolving needs. Grants

should be available only for construction which will accommodate increased numbers of students.

(2) College housing program. This program has been outstandingly successful in its 10 years of operation. It has suffered in uncertainty and needs to be put on a basis which will permit colleges and universities to plan ahead. The Task Force Committee therefore recommends that (a) the President ask Congress for an immediate increase in loan authorization of $150 million to take care of anticipated additional needs for the fiscal year ending June 30, 1961, and (b) the President ask Congress to increase the loan authorziation by $1.4 billion over a 4-year period, with $350 million of the new authorization available as of July, 1961, and $350 million on July 1, 1692, July 1, 1963, and July 1, 1964. (Program administered in Housing and Home Finance Agency.)

III. STRENGTHENING OF THE NATIONAL DEFENSE EDUCATION ACT

The need for action by the Federal Government to upgrade American education was clearly recognized in the passage by the Congress of the National Defense Education Act. In general the programs under the various titles have been effective and, with some modifications, the authority for them should be extended for 5 years.

Because of the critical shortage of teachers at all levels, highest priority should be given to enlarging the national fellowship program in order to attract able people into elementary and secondary, as well as college, teaching. New sources of supply should be tapped, such as college graduates, particularly women with lessened family responsibilities who did not specifically train to be teachers, retired military and other professional personnel. In addition, fellowships should be available to teachers in service so that they might increase their effectiveness.

The loan funds for college students should be increased and supplemented with a guaranteed loan program from private funds. The forgiveness feature, now applicable only to public school teachers, should be extended to all teachers. Furthermore, the student disclaimer affidavit which so many institutions find objectionable should be eliminated.

With the extensive experimentation which has been done throughout the country in the more effective use of newer means of communications in the schools, another phase should now be entered and assis-

tance given through Federal support to the States and regions in con-
structing educational television networks.

After 3 years of experience in granting aid to the States to develop
better means of identifying students with outstanding aptitudes and
encouraging them to complete their high school education, the time
has come to review carefully the work that has been done and to look
to the planning of programs that provide more thorough preparation
for vocational and academic counselors.

RECOMMENDATIONS FOR PRESIDENTIAL ADMINISTRATIVE ACTION

The Task Force Committee recommends immediate action by the
President with respect to four important matters listed below in order
or priority. The Committee believes the taking of these actions will
demonstrate in a positive way that the President not only gives top
priority to the development of the Nation's educational system, but
also stands ready to give his full backing to the establishment of helpful administrative policies and regulations in all Federal agencies
charged with the spending of Federal funds flowing to the colleges
and universities in support of education, research, and public service.

(1) The Task Force Committee recommends that the President
take immediate action to establish a President's Advisory Committee
on Education.

Such a move will demonstrate that the President believes that education is one of the truly fundamental and important requirements for
the preservation and development of the American society and will
place the field of education on a level with that now enjoyed by Presidential advisory groups in both science and economics.

(2) The Task Force Committee recommends that the President specifically request all Federal agencies, including the Federal Council for
Science and Technology, the National Science Foundation, the
Atomic Energy Commission, the Department of Defense, and the
Department of Health, Education, and Welfare, to take all possible
steps within existing statutory and legislative authorizations to support
and implement the recommendations of the President's Science Advisory Committee issued under date of November 15, 1960, in a report
entitled "Scientific Progress, the Universities, and the Federal Government."

This excellent report recommends objectives, policies, and actions
which will strengthen American science and technology the benefits

from which will serve to increase not only national defense, but also national industrial and economic growth.

The active implementation of these recommendations will be enthusiastically received by all institutions of higher learning in the country now concerned and faced with the problems of financing, staffing, and equipping an expanded capacity for graduate training and basic research.

(3) The Task Force Committee recommends that the President take action—presumably through the Secretary of the Treasury—to request the Internal Revenue Service to rescind Ruling 60-370, dated December 2, 1960.

The rescission of this ruling (which ruling has been vigorously opposed by all educational institutions, both public and private) will demonstrate that the new administration is anxious to do all in its power to stimulate private giving in support of our educational institutions.

(4) The Task Force Committee recommends that the President request the Director of the Bureau of the Budget to proceed with immediate revision of Bureau of the Budget Circular A-21, issued September 10, 1958, the intent of which is "to provide to educational institutions recognition of their full allocated costs of research under generally accepted cost accounting principles."

The revision of this directive will settle one of the most annoying problems in the field of university-Government relationships that has plagued our institutions of higher education for the past 10 years.

Specific recommendations on the changes desired were submitted to the Bureau of the Budget in September 1960 by a special committee on sponsored research of the American Council on Education, and to the Department of Defense and the three services.

7: CONSERVATION FRONTIERS

Because of the constructive commitments for resource development and conservation made by the President-elect during his campaign, we look forward to an administration that will establish landmarks of achievement toward a constructive program that will protect the rightful heritage of all Americans.

We know that vigorous new leadership is essential to conserve our renewable resources of water, soil and forests and that full development of these resources is necessary to make possible the growth of our economy essential to America's role in the free world. We believe that the widest enjoyment of benefits of our natural resources should be made possible for the greatest number of people at the lowest possible cost.

An adequate water supply for our growing population will be a major domestic need for many years to come. The physical needs of urbanism greatly accelerate this crisis. With such problems in mind, it is our recommendation that the new resource challenges of urbanism be met by closely coordinated Federal-State efforts. If a new Department of Urban Affairs is created, it should include within its framework a team of experts who can work with the regular resource agencies in meeting some of these problems.

Existing Federal agencies can do the necessary work for a meaningful conservation program. Conflicts between agencies can only serve to delay and defeat achievement of natural resource programs. Policy guidance can come from the President and a council of Resource and Conservation Advisors in the Office of the President.

Growing water needs make imperative the development of long-range research programs for the conversion of saline and brackish waters.

Research should also be pressed into improved methods for the construction of waterway projects. Full study should be given to the possibility of using nuclear devices for the construction of the projects and the recovery of minerals, including oil from shale.

Prepared under the direction of Rep. Frank E. Smith of Mississippi, Chairman of the Watershed Subcommittee of the House Committee on Public Works, this report was approved by an advisory committee composed of more than 200 persons.

BUDGETARY POLICY

We welcome the end of the "no new starts" policy. We believe that the national budget policy should distinguish between capital investment and operating expenditures in the natural resources field. The Bureau of the Budget should be used to measure the full benefits of projects in relation to the overall national economy and the national goals of all the people.

The restrictive interpretations of the Bureau of the Budget Circular A-47 should be ended at once. We believe that a re-study of the effect of this Circular should be ordered by the Bureau of the Budget and all provisions inconsistent with the stated goals of the Kennedy administration should be eliminated or changed. The "taxes foregone" calculation added into feasibility studies by A-47 is an example. Recreation benefits are becoming each year a more valuable part of every type of water project. These benefits should be included in the value of any type of federal water project. Recreational features should be utilized to the maximum in any type of federal water project and the value of these benefits should be included in the overall federal benefits of the project.

The tendency in recent years of the Bureau of the Budget to discourage any projects by excessive requirements for local interests should be modified to meet realistic water needs. Special consideration should be given to the problems of undeveloped and depressed areas.

FLOOD CONTROL AND RECLAMATION

Highest priority should be given to the completion of urgently needed flood control projects already authorized and earliest possible action should be taken toward authorization of projects that have been often delayed because of unreasonable Bureau of the Budget restrictions. We can never achieve the full development of our national economy until we have the assurance of flood protection of all of our river valleys. These projects are income-producing, wealth-creating assets, in addition to protecting lives and property.

The reclamation of land should be restored as an essential part of our natural resources program. The continued development of supplemental water supplies for existing irrigated acres and the opening of new lands for settlement through reclamation are entirely consistent with long-term national objectives. Such development provides a most important basic element to a successful regional economy, a stable diversified agriculture. The full development of our river basins carries with it not only flood control and reclamation benefits, but power, navigation and recreational dividends which contribute to the growing economy we seek.

WATERSHED DEVELOPMENT

Few resource programs can directly benefit as many citizens in as many States at so small a relative cost as the small watershed program. Beneficiaries of this program are not merely farmers, but millions of people in towns and cities. The recreational potential, largely unmeasured, will be invaluable to many more millions in the large urban areas. It could be one of the prime forces in bringing lasting help to economically depressed areas.

Already local organizations have applied for help in some 1400 watersheds containing about 100 million acres of land. Applications are falling off, however, because of the time lag before projects can be reached with the present limited planning funds.

Administration policy should include the following objectives:

(1) A goal of 2,000 watersheds completed or under construction by 1968.

(2) Completion by 1968 of the original pilot watersheds.

(3) Provision of adequate loan funds for local organizations.

(4) Organization of future years budgets so that resource conservation programs will be separated from unrelated activities. The small watershed program has been handicapped by competing for funds with the many other activities of the Department of Agriculture. It should be considered in relation to related programs of the Corps of Engineers, Reclamation, and other public works activities.

POWER

Long-range energy resource development objectives based upon forecasts of need and the public interest should be established by the federal government.

A national energy and fuels policy to guide federal agencies responsible for resource development should be enacted by Congress to provide:

(1) Progressive evaluation standards for multiple-purpose projects.

(2) Cost allocation formulae for multiple-purpose projects which are consistent with the principle of regulation by competition.

(3) Abundant electricity at minimum cost to the ultimate consumer, whether he is served by investor-owned, local public, or cooperative distribution systems.

The Department of the Interior, in cooperation with other agencies, must reassert its responsibility to provide long-range planning of generation and transmission facilities to meet future needs, with immediate attention to the economic necessity of inter-regional Federal transmission ties.

Regional wholesale power supply systems should be made responsible for meeting the expanding wholesale power requirements of all retail electric systems at the lowest possible cost and supplied with as much hydroelectric capacity as is economically feasible for low-cost peaking power and reserve capacity.

Falling water, coal at the mine mouth, atomic energy, or even solar energy could supply the fuel, depending upon conditions in various regions. Because our supplies of coal are plentiful and often more useful when converted to electricity, an important part of the power should be "coal by wire" from the now-depressed mining areas in West Virginia and Pennsylvania and the coal and lignite deposits of the West.

Atomic power, developed and financed by the people, should be made available from Federal nuclear power plants as soon as production costs can be materially reduced.

NAVIGATION

The waterways of the United States play a vital role in the economic strength and well-being of the nation. Their improvement and modernization constitute one of the most productive public investments highly rewarding to the American free enterprise economy. The freedom of the waterways from tolls or toll-equivalent charges or taxes is fundamental to their continued contribution to an expanding national economy.

Availability of low-cost water transportation provides a foundation for economic growth which could not occur on a comparable scale in its absence. It has generated a major post-war industrial expansion along the nation's navigable waterways, providing abundant opportunity for private investment, affording employment of a high productive character for hundreds of thousands of our people, and generating greatly enlarged productive capability for economic welfare and the national defense.

Navigation improvements have exhibited their values most strikingly in stimulating development of resources in regions of the country where growth has heretofore lagged through lack of economic access to markets and sources of raw materials. The rapid increase in tonnages of farm crops shipped by water has been substantially reducing the disparity between central market prices and income realization on the farm. Stimulus to water-dependent industry provided by improvements to harbors and waterways has been of especial benefit to regions suffering from the loss of traditional industries as a result of technological factors. By virtue of modernized water transportation, extensive areas of the nation have been contending successfully with the forces of economic stagnation and moving towards full participation in national standards of productivity and income.

The emerging problems of the future urgently demand a vigorous rededication to the philosophy of free waterways improvement. Considerations of national security, involving encouragement to dispersion of strategic industry, capabilities for low-cost mass transportation of basic industrial commodities and fuels, economy in the consumption of fuels and scarce materials and optimum recuperative power following heavy nuclear attack, also counsel an expanded program of waterways improvement.

The enormous growth of traffic on the waterway system in the post-war years is beginning seriously to over-tax its present capacity throughout extensive reaches. These deficiencies present a grave challenge to more purposeful direction of our national efforts. The demand for water transportation will probably double by 1980. Deficiencies in harbor and channel depths and inadequacies of locking facilities, many in advanced states of deterioration, are choking off development of water commerce and discouraging economies of deeper-draft, more powerful vessels. Many of our coastal harbors over the country are not prepared to handle deeper-draft vessels and a general program of modernization is needed.

Appropriate remedies for the consequences of past neglect and indifference call for full acceptance of Federal responsibilities for leadership in this vital area of the public domain, informed by recognition of the true public values involved. Failure to move forward with decisiveness on the construction of sound and productive projects can only result in the wanton neglect of our national capabilities at a time when every consideration of national interest dictates the intelligent and effective marshalling of all our resources.

POLLUTION CONTROL

One of the earliest enactments of the 87th Congress should be the Blatnik Pollution Control Bill, vetoed in 1960. In addition to financial assistance to local communities in the construction of sewage treatment facilities, necessary Federal enforcement, research and technical assistance programs should be strengthened.

National pollution policy should establish the goal as one which will protect and enhance the capacity of the water resource to serve the widest possible range of human needs. This goal can be approached only by accepting the positive policy of keeping waters as clean as possible, as opposed to the negative policy of attempting to crowd into a stream all the wastes it might possibly assimilate.

The policy should formally recognize recreation value of water resources as a full partner with domestic, industrial and agricultural values in water quality management and programs.

The administrative level of the water supply and pollution control activities in the Public Health Service and in the states should be commensurate with the importance of the problem.

Research into the use of highly toxic chemical pesticides, detergents as a destructive pollutant of land, water and air should be greatly expanded.

WILDLIFE CONSERVATION

We recommend Congressional passage of legislation which will assure perpetuation of wilderness values. A sympathetic administration can help eliminate confusion and misconceptions which have blocked passage of this legislation in the past. We need to protect specimens of our old frontier just as we need to protect national shrines and art treasures.

Wildlife refuges and ranges must be protected to serve the purposes to which they are dedicated without interference by commercial exploitation. Immediate legislative authorization is needed to establish a revolving fund for duck stamp revenue to permit immediate purchasing of wetlands before drainage destroys these areas. Cooperative programs should be developed to bring about the establishment of extensive wildfowl breeding grounds in Canada.

Production of fish in the lakes and wildlife on the perimeter of our reservoirs should become an integral part of reservoir manage-

ment. Research into fish production in Federal reservoirs is needed
to maximize benefits from them.

The many needs for work in reforestation, soil conservation, park
improvement and wildlife refuge work offers a potential for employment of several hundreds of thousands of idle young men between
the ages of 16-21 years. Both Federal and State projects could
utilize the work of high school "drop-outs" in need of work experience
and vocational training. Healthful outdoor work would improve
the level of physical fitness, reduce juvenile delinquency and generally
prepare more useful future citizens.

NATIONAL PARKS

Shoreline parks which should be made available for public recreation are the most critically needed additions to our national park
system. They must be acquired before all potential sites are lost
to urban development and commercial exploitation.

There is still great need for improving and expanding our national
park system to meet the needs of a greatly increasing population.
One solution which should be considered is a program of assistance
to states and local communities in the expansion of park resources.

FORESTRY

Increased attention to forestry—our great publicly-owned national
forests, the millions of small privately-owned forest tracts, forest
research—is one of the most meaningful investments we can make
in achieving the economic strength essential to our national goals.

If we are to meet our goals in wood fiber requirements in the next
40 years, our total production must be doubled. All forest land
ownership, government and private, will demand accelerated attention to meet this need. The greatest opportunity for improvement
is on the small, privately-owned, woodland tracts throughout the
country, which represent about half of our nation's total forest land.
Private credit sources are not available to the average small woodland owner for purchase and development of forested properties.
Expansion and liberalization of present government credit sources,
federal and state, tailored to meet the needs of the small owner are
needed until ready private credit sources develop. More research
is needed to show owners how their forest lands can be better
managed.

The cooperative forest programs conducted jointly by federal and state groups should receive the funds which have been denied over the past few years. The programs for our national forests badly need acceleration to meet existing needs.

Consideration should be given to the possibilities for expansion of the national forest system in depressed areas. Investments in our national forests yield direct returns to the taxpayers, as well as long-range benefits to our overall economy.

8: ADMINISTRATIVE FRONTIERS

INTRODUCTION

The general problem of the administrative agencies and their role in government has been a subject of consideration for the past twenty-five years by various branches of the government, bar associations and legal and political science scholars. These studies, extremely voluminous in character, have ranged over many topics from the fairness of the procedures employed in the adjudication of cases to the relationship that these agencies should bear to the Executive on the one hand and to the Legislative Branch of the Government on the other. Specific proposals for the internal reorganization or consolidation of various agencies have emanated from time to time and to a degree have become effective through legislation or through such powers as may have been delegated to the President under the various Reorganization Acts.

There has been no lack of concern with the general problem but, viewing the subject in the large, the concrete results achieved by these voluminous studies bear a very small ratio to the time and effort that the studies and investigations themselves have consumed.

Effective procedural solutions, so necessary to the proper functioning of the administrative agencies, have admittedly not been achieved despite the sweeping studies which culminated in the Administrative Procedure Act of 1946 and the many studies which have followed. Spectacular instances of executive, legislative and industry interference with the disposition of matters before the agencies have been uncovered. Expansion of the role, power and duties of the agencies has continued and despite the absence of effective solution of and increasing concern with their problems they now embrace within their regulatory powers almost every significant aspect of our national being.

Their continued existence is obviously essential for effective government. The complexities of our modern society are increasing rather than decreasing. The advent of atomic energy, of telecommunications, of natural gas, of jet aircraft, to cite only a few examples,

---

Report on regulatory agencies by James M. Landis, former Dean of the Harvard Law School and past chairman of the Securities and Exchange Commission.

all call for greater surveillance by government of the appropriate use of these resources to further the admittedly dim but recognizable aims of our society.

A reappraisal of the various functions and activities of the regulatory agencies is thus desirable at this very critical period of our national life for reasons that are only too apparent. The scope of responsibility entrusted to these agencies is enormous, exceeding in its sweep, from the standpoint of its economic impact perhaps, the powers remaining in the Executive and the Legislative. This is true despite the fact that such powers as they exercise are generally delegated to them by the Legislative. This delegation followed upon the conviction that the problems in a particular area were so manifold and complex that the Congress simply had neither the time nor the capacity to handle them. Similarly the delegation to them of adjudicatory powers stemmed from the conviction that the issues involved were different from those that theretofore had been traditionally handled by courts and thus were not suited for judicial determination. These delegations, once made, are rarely recalled or retracted; on the contrary, the tendency is to expand them as more and more complex problems arise. The legislative standards under which the delegations are made are similarly increasingly loosened so that not infrequently the guide in the determination of problems that face the agencies is not much more than their conception of the public interest.

This reappraisal to be of any value as a guide for action must have concreteness. Mere generalities will be useless. Nevertheless, absent generalizations that can be spelled out of facts, forward and constructive thinking is difficult. The experience of the past twenty-five years cannot be overlooked, nor can the existence of a problem in one agency be evaluated without the recognition that it has basic common aspects with like problems in other agencies. The approach, moreover, must be impartial in the sense that it should neither be a diatribe against the administrative process—a tendency characteristic of able but older scholars of the 1930's; nor should it have a bias in favor of the administrative disposition of matters, an attitude not uncommon among government servants too imbued with the bureaucracies that they administer.

Finally, it must be remembered that we cannot regard our government as simply a government of laws and not of men, but rather a government of laws by men. Although the mechanisms we create for administration may be more or less well adapted to a particular task, the individuals that operate them singly or as a group have the ultimate responsibility of guidance and control.

The results of their operations will thus reflect not only efficiency or inefficiency but more importantly the ideals and goals that within the framework of the basic law can fairly be achieved.

I. THE PROBLEM

There is no single solution which can be projected for problems common to all the regulatory agencies. Indeed, no one can even correctly define the term "regulatory agency," or enumerate the group that comes within such a concept. Classification of these agencies under the category of "independent" or "executive" is also meaningless. No rational line has been pursued by the Congress in differentiating the "independent" agencies from those embraced within some Executive Department. The regulation of stock exchanges, for example, has been delegated to an "independent" agency whereas the regulation of commodity exchanges is under the jurisdiction of an Executive Department. Similarly misrepresentation in the sale of articles, including drugs, is the concern of an independent agency, whereas so-called mislabelling of foods, drugs and insecticides, which reaches far beyond the mere label, is a concern of an Executive Department.

At various times in the last twenty-five years so-called general problems came to the surface. Twenty or more years ago the procedural aspect of administrative regulation and adjudication was the uppermost problem. The prime emphasis then was placed on the combination of prosecuting and adjudicatory functions within the same agency. It was the concern with this problem that led eventually to the passage of the Administrative Procedure Act of 1946 with its emphasis upon the internal separation of these functions within the agency and the granting of some degree of independence to the hearing examiners. It was the same emphasis that altered the pattern in 1947 of the National Labor Relations Board to deprive the Board of much of its power to initiate proceedings, transferring this function to an independent General Counsel—an experiment which after a decade of trial and error is not likely to be repeated.

Of late the emphasis has shifted to questions of conflicts of interest and *ex parte* presentations as well as to an effort to transfer certain adjudicatory functions to administrative tribunals or courts. The tendency here is again further to judicialize the administrative process and, in the opinion of many observers, to over-judicialize it to a point where stagnation is likely to set in. More recently a less legalistic approach has been taken, namely to treat the agency as more of a managerial mechanism so as to free it in its broader aspects from the burdens entailed by judicial requirements. This, for example, is the basic thought underlying such studies as those of Professor Emmette S. Redford of the University of Texas and those initiated through various management consultant firms by the Bureau of the Budget.

All of these have had their value and in their way have alleviated certain distressing tendencies becoming apparent on the administrative scene. Certain fundamental problems have, however, not been solved. On the contrary, their persistence is too serious to be longer ignored, for their prevalence is threatening to thwart hopes so bravely held some two decades ago by those who believed that the administration agency, particularly the "independent" agency, held within it the seeds for the wise and efficient solution of the many new problems posed by a growingly complex society and a growingly benevolent government. It is to these problems that this report addresses itself.

A. Delays in the Disposition of Adjudicatory Proceedings

Inordinate delay characterizes the disposition of adjudicatory proceedings before substantially all of our regulatory agencies. In the Civil Aeronautics Board, for example, the average age of dockets closed by formal proceedings in 1960 was some 32 months. As of June 30, 1959, out of 464 proceedings then pending, 166 had been pending for more than 3 years. The Federal Trade Commission as of June 30, 1959, had 309 cease and desist orders pending, of which 118 had been pending for more than one year and 30 for more than 3 years. In the Federal Power Commission the backlog of pending cases in 1959 was almost four times as great as in 1957. Only last September that Commission announced that it would take 13 years with its present staff to clear up its pending 2,313 producer rate cases pending as of July 1, 1960, and that with the contemplated 6500 cases that would be filed during that 13 year period it could not become current until 2043 A.D. even if its staff were tripled. Contested proceedings before the Interstate Commerce Commission tend to run from 18 to 36 months, and numerous proceedings before the Federal Communications Commission and the Maritime Board have been pending for more than 3 years. The statutory period

of 20 days during which a normal registration statement covering
the issuance of new securities becomes effective under the Securities
Act of 1933 has in practice been lengthened to some 40 to 60 days.
Numerous similar statistics can be gathered from other agencies,
including individual instances when even 10 and 14 years have elapsed
before a final determination has been made. They all corroborate
the fact of interminable delay.

The causes making for delay are not uniform. Some are due to
inadequate budgets. A period of economic rigor, if not parsimony
seems to have characterized the Bureau of the Budget's attitude
toward the various agencies beginning in 1952, an attitude that was
slowly being relaxed in 1960. During the fiscal year 1950, when 496
registration statements were filed with the Securities and Exchange
Commission, the Bureau of the Budget approved 1,130 employees
for the Commission, of which 1060 were authorized by Congress.
As of fiscal year 1955 with 849 registration statements filed with the
Commission, only 717 employees were approved by the Budget
Bureau, of which 699 were authorized by Congress. As of fiscal year
1960 with 1628 registration statements filed with the Commission
only 978 employees had been approved by the Budget Bureau, of
which 954 were authorized by Congress. Obviously either extrava-
gance characterized the situation in 1950 or parsimony in 1960. In
any event, the statutory waiting period during that decade was in
substance tripled. Similar situations prevailed in many other agencies.

The blame, if any, for this situation does not rest purely on the
Budget Bureau. The agency heads themselves, presumably under
the general direction of the Executive Office of the President, curtailed
their requests despite the growing pressure of the business pending
before them for disposition. Congress similarly exhibited the same
tendencies. Indeed, despite the decision of the Supreme Court of
the United States in the *Phillips* case in 1954 (347 U. S. 672) em-
powering in the Federal Power Commission to fix rates for producers
of natural gas and clearly envisaging a need for greatly expanded
personnel, a request for a supplemental appropriation of $300,000
was cut to $100,000.

Some causes for delay are peculiar to the particular agency. Following the *Phillips* case, the Federal Power Commission was flooded
with rate filings by the numerous producers of natural gas. In
general, these new rates were allowed to go into effect on the
condition that any reductions later determined by the Commission
should be refunded to the consumers. Since legislation was shortly

thereafter introduced to deprive the Commission of this aspect of its rate-making power, the Commission appears to have refrained from any real effort to deal with its docket on the theory that the passage of these bills, in the manner of a *deus ex machina*, would relieve them totally and finally of this sudden accretion in their business. The bills, however, were vetoed on two occasions and the problem in an immensely exaggerated form still rests on the door step of the Commission, since rate increase has now been pancaked upon rate increase. The consequences of this inaction have been serious, particularly to the individual natural gas consumers since, unlike the large industrial consumers, they cannot easily convert to a cheaper fuel and thus benefit from the restraint placed upon rising prices to industrial consumers by the existence of competitive fuel prices.

The situation in the Federal Communications Commission appears to derive from other causes, primarily the inability of that Commission to make up its mind on some of the broad issues that face it. Despite the patent failure evident by 1955 of the allocation system devised in 1952 to provide a viable economic life for users of the UHF frequencies in the same market, five years have now elapsed without any appreciable dent being made on this problem. True, during these years an extensive investigation was made by other sources of this problem, primarily by the Subcommittee on Communications of the Senate Committee on Interstate and Foreign Commerce. The Communications Commission, like the Federal Power Commission, may have hoped that some magic formula would spring from these investigations which would relieve it of the necessity for independent courageous action. If so, that hope was stillborn and the Commission's problem still remains. Here again delay has serious consequences on the destiny of television, for additional VHF channels have not been made available with the result that the existing monopoly of the established networks, particularly in the two TV channel markets, cannot economically be challenged by existing or potential programming entities. The recent action of the Commission in instituting a rule-making proceeding which may make available some VHF frequencies in one and two station markets may be something of a palliative to this situation but it is hardly a comprehensive answer.

The chief causes of these many delays, however, are the growing business before the regulatory agencies. Mere budget increases only occasionally will give an answer to this congestion. If these cases require disposition by the agency heads themselves, increases in the subordinate staff are not the answer. Far more searching answers are required, some of which are discussed at a later stage in this report. This is not to say that the agencies will not have before them over the years to come cases of complexity that will take years to conclude. But even with respect to these cases, measures to make less rather than more complex what is an inherently complex problem, must be devised.

B. Costs

Originally it was believed that a public benefit would ensue from the fact that the cost of pursuing an administrative remedy would be substantially less than the existing method of resort to the courts. This hope has not been realized except in those instances when the government itself has the duty in the public interest to pursue a remedy which otherwise would have had to be pursued by the private individual.

Studies as to the extent of these costs—strange as it may seem—have not been made. Apart from the costs to the individual petitioner, the costs to the government itself must be considered. The over-all costs themselves derive from two factors: first, the time element involved in waiting for an ultimate administrative determination and judicial review, if any, and, second, the length of the hearings that precede such a determination. Given a hearing with a record of some 20,000 pages, the costs merely of the acquisition of that record alone will total some $20,000. Additional costs in the preparation of numerous exhibits, the hiring of experts, such as engineers and accountants, fees paid to lawyers, and the expenses of housing and feeding this group of men during the weeks of hearings, bring the total to a very substantial sum. If some twenty or thirty participants or intervenors are involved in the proceeding, the overall cost becomes staggering. In the *Seven States Case* before the Civil Aeronautics Board, in which there were 150 parties and intervenors with 225 appearances noted and in which hearings lasted for 20 days, or the *Phillips Petroleum Co.* rate case before the Federal Power Commission in which 76 lawyers entered appearances for 33 parties and intervenors and in which the hearings consumed 82 days and oral argument before the Commission two further days, the total costs must have run into the millions. This latter case incidentally was only a later phase of proceedings initiated in 1948, and the decision recently made in 1960 is likely to be subjected to further review.

These examples of the scope of costs are not unusual. They mean that to be successful in a petition for an important certificate of public necessity and convenience or a television or radio license the petitioner must be well-supplied with funds, which the petitioner must be willing to wager on his chances of being successful. The result is that in many situations the small businessman is practically excluded from an opportunity to compete. A factor that tends to increase these costs is that in many cases they are passed on to the public in the form of rate increases or subsidies based upon their allowance as an operating expense, so that the companies lack any real incentive to cut them down.

A further element of costs in many situations is the resort to public relations techniques to create a national atmosphere congenial to the position of a particular petitioner or intervenor—an expensive operation—in the hope that such an atmosphere will produce a decision favorable to the applicant. On several occasions the larger airlines have resorted to this technique, as well as applicants for licenses or special privileges before the Federal Communications Commission. See e.g., *American President Lines*, 7 C.A.B. 799, 818; Proceedings subsequent to the decision in *United Airlines* v. *C.A.B.* 278 F. (2d) 446.

Indirect costs stemming from the factor of delay in the final determination can also assume large proportions. They are difficult to measure but from testimony recently adduced they can run into the millions with respect to a particular case. Delays in the issuance of pipe-line certificates by the Federal Power Commission have resulted in increased costs of from two to ten million dollars, costs that are inevitably passed on to the public. Delays in the establishment of rates for the transportation of gas are presently holding up programs for expansion which can involve over $100 million of steel construction, which in the light of the present employment of our steel capacity means much to the steel industry and the unemployment situation. Some $500 million is now held up under the suspension policy of the Federal Power Commission with reference to rates filed by natural gas producers, some of which is theoretically distributable to consumers but which practicably after the lapse of four to six years may never reach them. The delay in route cases before the Civil Aeronautics Board, such as the *Southern Transcontinental Route Case,* has held up procurement policies for commercial aircraft to an unknown degree. Delays in the time in which registration statements have become effective due to the burden of work before the Securities Exchange Commission have increased underwriting costs and forced resort to means of financing less desirable and more expensive.

C. PERSONNEL

It is generally admitted by most observers that since World War II a deterioration in the quality of our administrative personnel has taken place, both at the top level and throughout the staff.

The causes for this are complex. The years since 1946, despite the Korean War, have been years of relative complacency as contrasted with the period from 1933 to 1941. The fires that then fed a passion for public service have burned low, making recruitment an increasingly difficult task. Careful scrutiny of agency members from the standpoint of their qualifications as well as their prejudices in behalf of administering the legislative goals to which they were to be committed, was during these years too often replaced by a consideration of what political obligations could be repaid through appointments. The area of so-called Schedule C appointments, free from Civil Service requirements, was increased affecting seriously the morale of those persons who looked upon government service as a career. Advancements to choice positions were also less rarely made from the staff. Instead outsiders not infrequently less qualified were appointed to these positions.

These attitudes have had a serious impact upon the regulatory agencies. At the top level initial expertise would be lacking and the want of devotion to the public service militated against its acquisition through continuing tenure. Top administrative positions appear to have been sought frequently as stepping stones to further political preference or to positions of importance within the industries subject to regulation. A too common complaint at the bar is that the staffs have captured the commissions and that independent and bold thinking on the part of the members of these agencies is absent. These factors in turn reacted upon the staffs. Lacking challenges for creative effort, recruitment of outstanding younger men lagged perceptibly. Where in the 1930's a majority of the leading graduates of our better law schools chose public service, in the 1950's only a handful could be drawn away from the opportunities offered them by private practice. Even the spirit once displayed by the veterans of the early years ebbed through the absence of leadership at the top.

Two measures designed to cure this situation have failed to do so.

The first was a general and, indeed, generous increase in compensation payable, particularly at the top and bottom rungs. But even where salaries were made comparable in large measure to those paid by private industry this situation has not been corrected. The spark, the desire for public service, has failed of re-ignition.

A second measure, designed to afford a greater opportunity for leadership to the chairmen of our important Commissions has strangely missed fire. Prior to World War II, these chairmen were generally elected by the Commission members. Often the chairmanship was rotated year by year and, as in the case of the Federal Trade Commission and the Interstate Commerce Commission, the chairman becomes little more than the presiding officer at commission meetings. In other commissions the chairman took a position of leadership primarily through his personality, although possessing few powers other than those possessed by his colleagues. Since World War II, reorganization plans have allowed the President to appoint the chairman and have made the chairman responsible for the administrative direction and organization of his agency. The Interstate Commerce Commission, however, succeeded in arousing sufficient Congressional pressure to defeat the application of such a plan to it.

The obvious design of this provision of the various reorganization plans was to make the chairman the contact for agency affairs with the office of the President and, by enhancing his powers, to increase his prestige and to put him in a real position of leadership with reference to his agency. The measure has failed to achieve this purpose. Some chairmen, for fear of upsetting their colleagues, have not exercised the power delegated to them but referred responsibilities entrusted to them to the collective judgment of their colleagues. Some chairmen designated by the President have simply not had the qualifications or commanded the respect required to assume their rightful position. A device, that could have been of great value, has thus not been properly utilized.

D. ETHICAL CONDUCT

Much attention has recently been centered on efforts, unfortunately too frequently successful, to sway the judgment of the members of regulatory agencies by so-called *ex parte* approaches or arguments, usually personalized, made off the record in proceedings that should be decided on the record. The extent of these *ex parte* approaches has only partially been revealed. They come from various sources—the office of the President, members of the Congress, and the regulated industries. Some are made in good faith; others to further a personal desire regardless of the public interest. Many of them emanate from lawyers striving to press their clients' cause, indeed, one of the worst phases of this situation is the existence of groups of lawyers, concentrated in Washington itself, who implicitly hold out to clients that they have means of access to various regulatory agencies off the record that are more important than those that can be made on the record. These lawyers have generally previously held positions of more or less importance in the Government. The examination of the appointment diary of one of the present Commissioners gives strong inferential although not definitive proof of what these off-the-record approaches can imply.

One of the most extraordinary situations where these influences play a significant part—a situation technically legalized by the Civil Aeronautics Act—revolves about the White House itself. Under the Act the President has the ultimate determination as to which carriers shall fly what international and overseas routes. The grant of that privilege to the President was based on a conception that his responsibility for the conduct of foreign affairs and national defense might require some variations in such dispositions of these awards that the Civil Aeronautics Board might make. Since 1948, however, the decisions of the Board have been varied by the President in a manner that is definitely indicative of the exercise of power in ways never contemplated by the original Act. Although the approaches to the "White House" are necessarily shrouded in mystery, enough evidence exists to establish the fact that in this particular field "lobbying" in its worst sense was prevalent.

Instances have also recently been uncovered of actual malfeasance in the sense of bribery among high administrative officials. More serious than these are the subtle but pervasive methods pursued by regulated industries to influence regulatory agencies by social favors, promises of later employment in the industry itself, and other similar means.

Malfeasance to some degree will always characterize any human institution. The federal judiciary has not been immune from it. Laws exist which make malfeasance by administrators a crime and in the graver situations convictions of offenders have been obtained. The *ex parte* problem, however, is more insidious and more difficult to cope with. To shut off administrators from contact with the regulated industries except through formal proceedings is to restrict their means of gathering that very expertise that was the reason for the creation of the agency. To shut them off from persons, such as mayors and members of Congress, who are pressing for the public interest as they see it, is to keep them away from a grass roots exploration of what the needs of any segment of the public are. On the other hand, some restraints upon off-the-record approaches must be laced, in view of the fact that the extent of these has grown rather than lessened since World War II. Means of dealing with this problem are suggested in a later section of this report.

E. ADMINISTRATIVE PROCEDURES

Administrative procedures and practices have been a constant concern of the agencies themselves, the courts, the bar and scholars for a time long antedating World War II. Pleas for flexibility in these procedures characterized the situation in the early 1930's. Application of even lax rules of evidence to administrative proceedings, particularly when they were being conducted by laymen, was thought undesirable. Commingling of the prosecuting and adjudicatory functions was deemed not only necessary but advisable.

A reaction to these tendencies set in during the latter part of that decade. Records had become unduly long, causing expense and delay. Procedures unchecked by basic requirements other than loose concepts of due process varied from agency to agency bringing a sense of confusion into the entire administrative process. The combination of the functions of prosecutor and judge, especially in the hands of laymen, developed a belief that elements of fairness were too frequently absent. Courts through their exercise of the power of judicial review sought to remedy some of these matters but the cures suggested frequently only increased the difficulties faced by the agencies in disposing of the business that confronted them.

Beginning about 1938 concerted efforts were made to deal with these problems. At the outset, spurred on by an antagonism to the very powers exercised by the regulatory agencies, the bar as a whole sought to impose the straight-jackets of traditional judicial procedure on the agencies. They were countered by other forces which sought to retain the value of the administrative process but still advocated reforms that would assure fairness in the exercise of powers delegated to the agencies. Some eight years thereafter a compromise between these two opposing views was effected by the enactment of the Administrative Procedure Act of 1946. That Act, however one may evaluate it, is far from a definitive solution of the problems with which it dealt. It has achieved some uniformity of procedure, some assurance of the application of fairer standards, but with its emphasis on "judicialization" has made for delay in the handling of many matters before these agencies.

Revisions and amendments to the Administrative Procedure Act are a constant and continuing concern of both the bar and the government. This is bound to continue and it is good that it should continue. No single mind and no group of minds can in any short period of time grapple with all the complexities of administrative procedure and bring forth a reasonably definitive code. This is a problem which has to be tackled piece by piece and year by year by men who have a continuing concern with its ever-changing phases. No "Hoover Commission" or "Advisory Committee" established other than on a continuing basis can hope to evolve those procedures that should govern the many different problems that the various regulatory agencies face. The traditional concepts themselves are elusive. Rate-making, for example, has as many different facets as a diamond. In the regulation of railroad rates considerations are present that are wholly different from the regulation of rates for electric power or the transmission of gas or oil. Air passenger fares and air freight rates present variant problems due in part to the rapid obsolescence of equipment. Rates for natural gas producers pose an entirely different story. The attempt to analogize these methods through a common concept of a rate of return on invested capital has a more theoretical than realistic basis. Procedures for the discovery of the facts upon which these differing judgments must be made cannot (and should not) necessarily be uniform.

Very recently suggestions have been advanced that due to modern techniques for the assemblage of facts, the older "judicialized" forms may well be supplanted. The exact technology applicable to such a process has not as yet been clearly articulated. But if judgments of regulatory agencies in many fields such as rates are, in truth, business judgments rather than judgments conforming to a legal theory, techniques which do not rest upon the tedious process of examination and cross-examination and which underlie honest business judgments made by the industries may have a value in the handling of substantially the same problem by the agencies. Indeed, in certain areas of transportation, the issue no longer is a fair rate of return on invested capital but how much the traffic can bear since the public interest requires the economic survival of the particular means of transport. Minimal and, perhaps, subsidized rates will be the most recurring issue, rather than the determination of maximal rates which was required in an age of non-competing modes of transportation.

F. ADMINISTRATIVE ORGANIZATION

Akin to the problem of administrative procedure is that of the organization of the regulatory agencies. Various general proposals have been made during the past few years. One of the most radical, recently pressed by a former member of the Civil Aeronautics Board, is a separation of their "policy" functions from the adjudicatory functions. These "policy" functions would be transferred to an executive department, leaving the adjudicatory functions with the commission members. The commission as a body is said to be incapable of policy making since it is required to adopt the wrong procedures, namely quasijudicial methods, to formulate policy.

Admittedly, many of the commissions have neglected their planning or creative functions. This is due in large part to the burden of the routine business thrust upon them and also to the calibre of appointment which have, however, on occasion been carried on effectively by commissions. The specialist study by the Securities and Exchange Commission, its unlisted trading study, its examination of corporate reorganizations, its investment company study, its examination of corporate trustees, the public utility holding company study of the Federal Trade Commission, its basing point study, the international route study of the Civil Aeronautics Board, are all examples of effective studies and planning undertaken by commissions, all of which have eventuated in basic national policies. "Policy" is also formulated in the process of decision making, as witness the differentiation of private versus public offerings of securities or the contrasting roles of trunk and local service carriers. Decision making, however, throws up issues less rarely as a result of deliberate planning and most frequently as a result of the incidence or accidence of cases or controversies. Policy also emanates from rule-making where forward-planning is more possible as, for example, the current effort of the Securities and Exchange Commission to fit so-called variable annuities into the existing pattern of regulation of financial mechanisms designed to absorb the people's savings.

The real issue is not whether the planning function should be delegated to an executive or to a commission but whether the individuals entrusted with such a responsibility have the capacity and the time with which to discharge it. A subsidiary issue is whether the individuals to whom such a function is entrusted are free to use flexible procedures in the search for ideas and policies, or are bound either as a matter of routine or law to pursue procedures ill-adapted for the performance of such a function. In both respects many of our commissions suffer. On the other hand, they can bring to the process of planning a wealth of information and knowledge based upon their experience and their realization of the practical limits of administrative action. These qualities are important as contrasted with planning functions performed in the isolation of an ivory tower.

Some functions that are more truly planning than adjudicatory have been forced too rigidly into the latter mould. This is true of the grant of air line certificates, of licenses for radio and TV transmission, of the reorganization and recapitalization of utility holding companies, of the issuance of pipe line certificates and of rate making in general. The cure here is not the transfer of these functions to an executive department but the adoption and initiation of procedures more suited to deal with the problems they present.

Indeed, some such transfers of these functions have not proved to be too successful. No policy, not even a discernible pattern, has emerged from the President's handling of international air routes and air carriers. Considerable controversy attends the promulgation of rules by the one-man Federal Aviation Agency without following procedures that admit of participation by the various segments of the industry in their formulation. The planning now centered in the General Counsel of the National Labor Relations Board by virtue of his control over the initiation of complaints, has in the opinion of many observers been more of a hit and miss operation than a comprehensive and cohesive approach to a difficult problem.

Generalizations as to the organization of administrative agencies are not only difficult but dangerous to make. One generalization, however, can safely be made. Unlike the judges of the federal judiciary, members of administrative commissions do not do their own work. The fact is that they simply cannot do it. In adjudicatory matters, the drafting of opinions is delegated to opinion writing sections or assistants so that the rationalization upon which a purportedly informed decision rests is truly their own. One can well imagine the morass which would characterize our constitutional law dealing with "due process" had the Justices of the Supreme Court for the last half century had their opinions drafted by clerks and issued anonymously. Who could then assay the work or the philosophy of a Holmes, a

Brandeis, a Hughes or a Cardozo? Yet, this is substantially the state of the law emanating from the thousands of decisions issued by the Civil Aeronautics Board, the Interstate Commerce Commission, the Securities and Exchange Commission, the Federal Power Commission and the National Labor Relations Board. But worse than this, it is a general belief, founded on considerable evidence, that briefs of counsel, findings of hearing examiners, relevant portions of the basic records, are rarely read by the individuals theoretically responsible for the ultimate decision. It is difficult for them to do otherwise, for as the analysis of the work load of one commissioner indicated, he had to make a decision during his work-day every five minutes, or as another commissioner recently testified, he made 18,000 decisions in five years. The fact is that delegation on a wide scale, not patently recognized by the law, characterizes the work of substantially all the regulatory agencies and certainly all the major ones. Absent such delegation, the work of these agencies would grind to a stop.

The real issue that we face is whether to recognize openly this fact of delegation or continue with the present facade of non-delegation, which prevents administrators from doing the work for which they have been appointed. There are answers to this problem as will be indicated later but they entail broad changes in the presuppositions that the public has been led to believe underlies the work of our regulatory agencies.

Apart from this generalization and its implications, it is unsafe to speculate broadly upon the appropriate organization of the regulatory agencies. The architectural design fit for a railroad station may be totally unfit for an air line terminal and certainly unusable as a marine dockyard. There are, of course, stresses and strains in any structure and the mathematical laws governing their computation are uniform, but the agencies have to be shaped internally for the functions that they are intended to serve. The Bureau of the Budget has in recent years engaged a series of management consultant firms to make studies of the major agencies at a cost of some $290,000. These studies vary greatly in quality and may be criticized on the ground that their conclusions lack a certain degree of independence. Since these consultants are presumably experts in the esoteric art of management rather than experts in the field covered by the agency or in administrative procedures, they are limited in their scope to the management side of the agencies rather than being concerned with the substantive character of their operations. Whether a hearing examiner spends two days or two months in the preparation of his findings is less important than the quality of the final product and that quality is not measurable by mechanical means.

These management studies are of varying quality and disparate value. They may in some situations ease bottlenecks and streamline the operations of departments that have become mired in outworn routines. It is, perhaps, too early to assess the impact of these studies. There is considerable opinion that the Howrey "reorganization" of the Federal Trade Commission, following the lines recommended by the management consultants and contrary to those recommended by the Hoover Commission in 1950, has been productive of delay rather than expedition. Also the concept of the executive director, which has been adopted by some of the commissions and which runs through most of these reports, has yet to become crystallized and prove itself. A chief assistant to a chairman, provided that the chairman has the responsibility to handle the administrative aspects of the agency's work, seems less presumptuous and appears to work better. Persons with grandiose titles tend to assume grandiose powers and forget that a chairman with respect to his colleagues and almost as much with respect to important departmental heads must give the impression that he is *primus* but only *inter pares*.

Follow-up surveys should, of course, be conducted to determine what recommendations have been adopted and proved themselves as well as what recommendations have been rejected. The responsibility of the Bureau of the Budget in this respect should not be sporadic but continuing and should itself make some evaluation of the recommendations submitted by the management consultants.

G. The Formulation of Policy Within the Agency

A prime criticism of the regulatory agencies is their failure to develop broad policies in the areas subject to their jurisdiction. As this report noted earlier policy formulation can be made in various ways including the adjudicatory process. The failure to utilize other methods for policy formulation is due primarily to the pressure of business on the adjudicatory side.

"Policy formulation", unless required by the disposition of a particular case, means planning measures as how best to dispose of pending problems or how best to forecast and explore solutions to problems still on the horizon. In the former field there are outstanding failures such as the allocation problem in the television field and rate regulation of natural gas producers. A series of other hiatuses in various regulatory fields can be mentioned, arising out of the inability to fashion viable patterns through the process of adjudication. Thus, the licensing of television and radio stations forms no decipherable pattern to permit the adjudicatory process to be both fairly and relatively easily exercised. The certification of air carriers on particular routes presents the same picture. Enforcement of the Robinson-Patman Act, due to the vagaries of the basic legislation, suffers from the same fault. In areas such as these where the case-by-case method has failed to pick out decipherable patterns and create "policies," other methods of policy planning are required.

Where, however, the greatest gaps exist are in the planning for foreseeable problems. Absent such planning the need for *ad hoc* solutions to the particular manifestations of the problem precede and, indeed, may preclude any basic policy formulation. The duty to undertake such planning is set forth with considerable specificity in many of the basic statutes creating the agencies, and yet plans have failed to evolve. Transportation is the most obvious of these areas. Planning to deal with the inevitable impact of increased competition on both long-haul and short-haul freight and passenger rail transportation has been minimal. Bureaucratic obstacles to the abandonment of unprofitable inter-city service became so severe and so unrealistic that the Transportation Act of 1958 sought in a way, perhaps too severely, to cut the Gordian knot. The problems of the shorter-haul carrier, such as the New Haven Railroad, could be seen long in advance but plans to deal with the problem as such have not yet been devised. The general deterioration of rail service, particularly on the Eastern roads, goes on apace, yet its tie-in with rates and financing is still to be determined. Such solutions as have been devised are piecemeal in character and bold and imaginative thinking is lacking. Commodity tariff classifications still reflect an economy whose changes have made many of them obsolete. In aviation much the same is occurring. The impact of the jet plane, substantially tripling the capacity of propeller-driven aircraft on our domestic and international route structures has received no serious consideration despite the obvious threat that the advent of the jet poses for the position of many of our intermediate trunk carriers. Instead of forward route planning the CAB now finds itself faced with potential mergers that under the pressure of financial exigency may force changes in route patterns and route structures far different from those that might otherwise have been deemed desirable. With planes with a March 2 speed already on the drawing boards planning far beyond the now conventional jet is necessary. Re-evaluation of our theories of international air rights and routes should similarly be now in process. In the maritime field, due to new competitive forces and the changing patterns of world commerce, re-examination must constantly be made of our subsidy policies which may be producing uneconomic competition on over-expanded trade routes in foreign commerce. Indeed, the impact of subsidy in many fields calls for re-examination of existing goals. Until World War II, the conception of the airplane as a commercial transport was limited to passengers and mail. Its adaptation, particularly since the advent of the jet, to extensive air cargo operations may well be more valuable from a national standpoint than the $60,000,000 to $80,000,-000 now being paid annually to keep our local service airlines alive. Time spent on a problem such as this can well be more rewarding to the public interest than on an issue as to whether cities X and Y should be interlinked by more passenger air service.

H. INTER-AGENCY POLICY FORMULATION

If there is lack of policy formulation within agencies, there is an almost complete barrenness of such formulation for those matters with which groups of agencies are concerned. The few inter-agency committees that have been set up have accomplished too little in conducting their separate approaches to a common problem. The most successful, the Air Coordinating Committee, proved so unsuccessful in dealing with the major problem of air space control that its function in this respect had to be turned over by the Federal Aviation Act of 1958 to a single agency, the Federal Aeronautics Administration.

There are many areas calling for well coordinated attacks upon problems common to many agencies. This is true in the fields of transportation, communications, energy, monopoly, and unfair trade practices. The development of a national transportation policy, as urged in the Democratic platform of 1960, calls for the achievement of maximum efficiency in transport, which, in turn means that "at a given level and structure of capital investment, efficiency requires that traffic be distributed among motor carriers, railroads, water carriers, pipelines and air carriers in such a way that each type receives the traffic which it can carry with the best consumption of resources by the carrier for the service standards required by the user. It requires also that several forms of transport be used in coordination where such a combination can produce a better service-cost result than any single form working alone. Finally it requires that every enterprise participating be ably and energetically managed." See Williams and Bluestone, *Federal Transportation Policy and Program*, p. 2.

The prime Federal Agencies concerned with the development of such a policy are the ICC, the CAB, the FMB, the FPC, the Bureau of Public Roads, the Military Transportation Service, the Army Corps of Engineers and the Department of Commerce. With reference to some phases of transportation it will also become necessary to effect coordination with various state and municipal agencies in order to deal with problems of a local or regional nature.

The inability to effect inter-agency coordination has been responsible for the lack of any policy as to the nature of the competition that should exist as between forms of transportation and also as between the carriers themselves. Military transportation, as presently conducted, competes heavily with commercial transportation, and there are patent abuses that attach to the government as a mass shipper, but it still insists on going its own way regardless of the effects its policies may have upon other carriers. Improvement of our rivers continues at the expense of the railroads, who are given the dubious privilege of reducing their rates to meet this new competition. The commutation crisis that was apparent a decade ago has had little or no effective help from the Federal Government despite some rather casual and ineffectual investigations by the Interstate Commerce Commission. The only remedy thus far devised has been periodic increases in commutation rates, a seemingly endless process since the causes that make for deterioration remain unchecked. Despite the tremendous decreases in rail passenger movements and their increasing cost the defeatist observation of the Interstate Commerce Commission examiners to this general problem to the effect that the passenger railroad car is likely to be found only in a museum in the 1970's is not likely to become true. User charges based upon use of federal facilities or federally subsidized facilities are unevenly distributed among the various forms of transportation thus favoring one form of transportation against another, and imposing upon the tax-payer costs properly chargeable to others.

It is unnecessary to catalog further the many different areas of interaction and the achievements that might be accomplished were an articulate national transportation policy to be ground out by the process of coordination. Thus strengthening our transportation system for peacetime purposes mean much for it can that much more effectively respond to wartime needs.

Communications presents a second area where effective interagency

action is lacking. Present communication policy making machinery
was established in 1934 in the context of regulating a private industry, and before the advent of radar, television, jet aircraft, intercontinental rockets, space communications and radio astronomy. Since
then new demands from industry, new needs in international telecommunication and new means of communication have created a
situation where the coordination of various endeavors must be effec-
tuated if we would deal with communications effectively in the national
interest. This is particularly true in the cold war environment of the
1960's which calls upon us to utilize every resource available in the
telecommunications field in our struggle not merely for prestige but
for survival.

Many agencies have a concern with the problems in this area. They
include the Federal Communications Commission, the State Department, the National Aeronautics and Space Administration, the Inter-
departmental Radio Advisory Committee of the Office of Civil and
Defense Mobilization, the Army, the Navy, the Air Force, and the
Federal Aeronautics Administration. The problems are many and
complex. They involve the allocation of both radio and television
frequencies as between Federal and non-Federal uses—an allocation
that has not been satisfactorily solved and whose present solution en-
tails increasing difficulties in the international field as new nations, presently neutrals but hopefully our allies, are pressing for frequencies in
the high frequency band for domestic communications and to express
their personalities on the air waves of the world. Redistribution of
spectrum space internationally is almost certainly in the offing and
its effect upon our vital communication facilities, both Federal and
non-Federal, must be considered. Modern developments in space
telecommunications, as set forth in two reports dated March 19, 1960,
and December 4, 1960, to the Senate Committee on Aeronautical and
Space Sciences point up the possibilities of substantial augmentation
of our presently limited intercontinental communications through
communication satellites, thus relieving our present dependence on the
limited high frequency band. Mechanisms for the effective exploration and utilization of this augmented spectrum must be developed in
an atmosphere far broader than that allotted to and operable by any
single existing agency. Only a closely coordinated combination of
the appropriate agencies concerned with this problem can make
such mechanisms possible.

The necessary coordination today is non-existent. The Federal
Communications Commission expends substantially all its energies

on the handling of problems relating to public broadcasting. The Telecommunications Division within the State Department entrusted with international telecommunication relationships is several layers deep within the Department. It has been permitted to decline in expertness, leadership, activity in international matters, as well as personnel. The International Radio Advisory Committee has a responsibility with reference to Federal and non-Federal frequency allocations but each government body makes its own allocations within the areas allotted to it, so that apportionment of the radio spectrum is a matter of *ad hoc* negotiation rather than of planned usage. There exists also a Presidential telecommunications adviser whose many other duties frequently overshadow telecommunications. Other committees are advisory to executive departments or offices such as the Telecommunications Coordinating Committee, the Telecommunications Advisory Board and the Telecommunications Planning Committee. But no general over-all coordination exists out of which broad national policies can emerge.

Studies pointing up the lack of this coordination and suggesting various means to cure that lack have been carried on for some 10 years. Bills to create a new authority with wide powers have been introduced from time to time in the Congress, and have generally met severe opposition from the Executive Department. Hearings upon a similar bill introduced this year have already evoked the strong opposition of the Department of Defense.

Energy is another area where interaction is essential and where substantially none exists. If we would increase our energy resources and utilize them wisely, coordination both as to utilization and conservation is essential. Various departments and agencies have a concern with segments of this problem. Surface transportation of oil, coal and liquified gas lies within the purview of the Interstate Commerce Commission and the Federal Maritime Board, and surface transportation of fuels is of enormous consequence in view of the importance of transportation costs in the pricing of the product. Natural gas is a concern of the Federal Power Commission. Electric power in its various forms falls within the purview of the Federal Power Commission, the Department of the Interior, the Corps of Army Engineers, the Tennessee Valley Authority and similar entities. The derivation of energy from fissionable materials is the business of the Atomic Energy Commission. General concern over the conservation of resources from which energy is developed rests primarily with the Department of the Interior, whereas the State Department and the Tariff Commission are factors in dealing with the extent to which our foreign investment is concerned with the production of fuel abroad as well as the extent to which these fuels should enter the domestic market.

Government actually controls to a considerable extent the degree to which these fuels are competitive and the exercise of these controls can affect to a great degree the rate of consumption of our resources. Indeed, the rate at which our own resources of natural gas are being tapped to a point where within a foreseeable period they may be exhausted is, in the opinion of many, a worrisome problem. But the coordination of policies with regard to their use and their conservation has not developed; indeed, an over-all concern with these questions has hardly been evidenced.

Perhaps more important than this is the matter of the continued development of other sources of energy. In this area the hydrogenation of coal and oil-bearing rock is outstanding. In the opinion of many an all-out national effort similar to that which has harnessed atomic energy might well solve this problem in such a way that we might not need to concern ourselves with sources of energy for another hundred years. But inter-agency mechanisms for planning or even suggesting such projects are absent.

Still other areas point up the need for coordination or the elimination of overlapping jurisdictions. Chief among these are the areas of monopoly and unfair trade practices. In the former the Federal Trade Commission and the Department of Justice have an overlapping jurisdiction, although they employ different sanctions to achieve their results. Some concern with the problems of monopoly are also the concern of the Interstate Commerce Commission, the Civil Aeronautics Board, the Federal Power Commission and the Federal Communications Commission. Sanctions possessed by the Department of Justice appear over the years to be more effective and more expeditious than are employed by the Federal Trade Commission. In the field of unfair trade practices, particularly false advertising, there is also an overlap between the Federal Trade Commission and the Food and Drug Administration now under the Department of Health Education and Welfare. Efforts to resolve this jurisdictional conflict were undertaken without success in 1933-1934 and have intermittently been tackled since. A possibility of conflict also exists in the field of insecticides and fertilizers between the Food and Drug Administration and the Department of Agriculture, subsidiary phases of which recently came to light during the recent notable cranberry episode. Jurisdictional lines inevitably dim at different points, but where the overlapping jurisdictions are patent, concurrent and uncoordinated regulation can evolve differing policies as well as produce unnecessary expense and bureaucratic waste.

I. THE RELATIONSHIP OF THE AGENCIES TO THE EXECUTIVE

The relationship of the agencies to the Executive has never been appropriately defined. It probably cannot be, but the shadows that now surround it can to a degree be lifted. In this respect there is not too great a difference between the allegedly "independent" agencies and those technically a part of some Executive Department. The President's arbitrary interference would be subject to resentment equal to that engendered by a similar interference with the Securities and Exchange Commission. The same would hold whether it involved Food and Drug Administration or the Federal Trade Commission. Whatever relationship can be spelled out as appropriate for the independent agencies, such a relationship would *a fortiori* hold for the other agencies.

The independent agencies are clearly dependent upon the Executive in four respects. The first is, of course, in the matter of appointments at the commissioner level. The degree to which they are subject to removal at the pleasure of the President is not uniformly clear. When the statute prohibits their removal except for cause the President's power of removal is limited to "cause", *Humphrey's Executor* v. *United States*, 195 U.S. 602 (1934). But there is no suggestion as to the extent to which judicial review could be had over a finding of "cause" by the President. Where no such prohibitions exist in the statute, a similar limitation may, however, be read into the statute for appointees who exercise quasi-judicial duties. *Cf. Wiener* v. *United States*, 357 U. S. 349 (1958).

A second definite relationship exists between these agencies and the President in that the Bureau of the Budget controls the budget submitted by the agency to the Congress and the agency is expected to support this budget. This does not mean that the Congress may not appropriate sums to the agency in excess of those approved by the Bureau, but in practice such over-appropriations are rare. The President thus through his practical control over agency expenditures can affect very substantially the emphasis placed by the agency on certain of its activities.

A third relationship arises out of the fact, now generally acknowledged although at one time contested by Commissioner Eastman of the Interstate Commerce Commission, that no legislative proposal shall be submitted by the independent agencies to the Congress unless they have been cleared through the Bureau of the Budget. This restriction also applies to other than casual comments made by the agency on bills pending before the Congress.

The fourth relationship arises out of the fact that, except for the Interstate Commerce Commission, the President appoints from among the agency members a chairman with more or less general administrative power. The situation with respect to the Federal Power Commission is somewhat confused in this respect due to a palpable error in the drafting of the reorganization plan covering that agency. The appointed chairman presumably is the avenue of contact between the agency and the President although this has not always been the case.

Other less tangible relationships exist. For some years now the Bureau of the Budget has concerned itself with the administrative management of the various major agencies. This concern has grown in recent years to the point where the Bureau has engaged outside managerial consultants to survey the major agencies. Subsequent surveillance as to the effectiveness of these surveys in bringing about managerial improvements is being undertaken. The Bureau of the Budget is thus quietly and unassumingly becoming in essence a Bureau of Administrative Management, to the functions of which it could, if it so chose, attach powerful sanctions.

Consultations may occur with more but usually with less frequency between the President and the chairman or members of the agency. The absence of national politics picked out by the agencies and the complexity involved in the handling of any national problem due to its Balkanization among a series of agencies makes worthwhile consultations of this type rare and consequently infrequent. A device has thus grown up in the past two administrations of delegating these agency and inter-agency problems to one or more "White House assistants". This procedure has had its shortcomings. These assistants have either not had the knowledge or the prestige to be effective in handling agency chairmen and members, especially those in the "independent" category; or, if the assistant possesses the prestige sufficient to qualify him popularly as an "Assistant President" he tends to overstep the bounds of his authority and tends to interfere in the disposition by the agency of individual cases. A reference to the interference of Sherman Adams in the Dixon-Yates matter or to the Murray (Chotiner)—Sherm (Adams) correspondence in the North

American Airlines case pending before the Civil Aeronautics Board is sufficient to illustrate this point.

There is an obvious necessity for the President to keep abreast of such national policies as may or may not be in the making or the handling or failure to handle national problems of national impact. He has also the constitutional duty to see that the laws are faithfully executed and this duty is applicable to the execution of laws entrusted to regulatory agencies, whether technically "independent" or not. The patent failure of the Federal Power Commission to execute the laws relating to natural gas production is thus rightly a matter of constitutional concern to him. As to this failure the Circuit Court of Appeals of the District of Columbia recently on December 8, 1960, had this to say:

"We believe that the Supreme Court [in the *Catco* case] meant to impress upon the Commission an interpretation of the "public interest" which, in the context of a rising natural gas market, demands a real administrative effort to hold back prices. We find nothing in the record before us which would justify the conclusion that the Commission had adequately performed this duty."

Whether such failure adequately to perform a statutory duty would be "cause" for removal is a question as to which lawyers might argue but which from the practical governmental stand-point permits of only one answer.

The congestion of the dockets of the agencies, the delays incident to the disposition of cases, the failure to evolve policies pursuant to basic statutory requirements are all a part of the President's constitutional concern to see that the laws are faithfully executed. The outcome of any particular adjudicatory matter is, however, as much beyond his concern, except where he has a statutory responsibility to intervene, as the outcome of any cause pending in the courts and his approach to such matters before the agencies should be exactly the same as his approach to matters pending before the courts.

Delegation of his constitutional responsibilities in this area is obviously essential, but, on the basis of past experience the device of one or more "White House assistants" is not the answer.

J. RELATIONSHIP OF THE AGENCIES TO THE LEGISLATIVE

The relationship of the agencies to the Congress generally speaking is that of any statutory branch of the Executive to the Congress, with certain exceptions. Oversight of their activities is naturally a concern of the Congress. But with respect to their quasi-judicial functions they should have the same immunity as courts. This does not mean that the Congress should not inquire into any improprieties in their quasi-judicial behavior. In this respect the opportunity of inquiry is, perhaps, greater than with respect to federal judges, but, given no impropriety, the rationality of their decisions or their attitude towards the handling of pending cases, even though some of them may not yet have reached the adjudicatory stage, should not be subject to inquiry. Their independence in this respect should be as much respected as that of the judges.

Their responsibility is to the Congress rather than solely to the Executive. The policies that they are supposed to pursue are those that have been delineated by the Congress, not by the Executive. Departure from these policies or the failure to make them effective or their subordination of legislative goals to the directions of the Executive is thus a matter of necessary legislative concern.

There is no question but that Congress has both the right and duty to inquire into effectiveness of the operation of the regulatory agencies and their handling of the broad powers that have been delegated to them. The real issue is the capacity of the Congress to keep abreast of the programs and the policies being carried out by these agencies.

In this respect Congress is faced with the same difficulties that attach to the Executive, namely the need to delegate its responsibilities in the face of other demands on its time and the difficulties of evaluating the basic national problems involved because of the many agencies dealing with them. The agencies touch the Congress, at least at two points— the Appropriations Committee and the appropriate committee, such as the Committees on Interstate and Foreign Commerce, having jurisdiction over their subject matter. Since the Legislative Reorganization Act of 1946, these committees have been furnished with better and more competent staffs. This is a definite help and enables the Committee to pierce the self-serving testimony normally adduced from the agencies. Relatively substantial improvement has thus occurred in this field, but more is needed. The committee staffs are often not too competent or have such short lives that they cannot become too familiar with the complex problems facing the major agencies. It is not easy quickly to evaluate the competency and efficiency of any particular agency especially when its activities fail to give an integrated picture.

Usually these investigations or hearings are sporadic in nature having been sparked by some incident that has caught the attention of the press. Regular surveys of their activities would be far more valuable. Usually their annual reports, always too self-serving, suggest some change in their basic statutes and this request for legislative aid gives a good ground for a survey of their past record. Annual or even biennial committee examination, based upon thorough prior preparation, would permit the Congress to have a better knowledge of the calibre of their personnel and the manner in which they are discharging their responsibilities.

II. Suggested Remedies

These then are the major problems that face our growingly important scheme of administrative regulation. It is not possible to deal with all these problems either administratively, by executive action or by legislation. They will require the use of every method, but executive action promises more expeditious handling of many of them. The fact is that during the last decade the Executive appears to have had no real concern with their operation. True, beginnings have been made to survey their capacity to manage their business, in keeping track of their operations through the accumulation of statistics by the establishment of an office of Administrative Procedure in the Department of Justice, in stimulating conferences on administrative procedure, in studying some of the elements essential to the development of a national transportation policy, and in advancing the career service of the hearing examiners. But such advances have been nullified by the appointment of members of these agencies on political grounds, and by not advancing to posts of signifiance within the agencies men experienced by long service in their business. Largely on political grounds, outsiders lacking necessary qualification for their important tasks have been appointed. There has also been too much of the morale-shattering practice of permitting executive interference in the disposition of causes and controversies delegated to the agencies for decision. Never before recent times in the history of the administrative process have the federal courts been compelled to return administrative decisions to the agencies, not because they have erred, but because they have departed from those fundamentals of ethics that must characterize equally the performance of quasi-judicial and judicial duties. Cancers such as these sweep through the entire process, dulling the sense of public service and destroying the confidence that the public must repose in public servants.

A. DELAY, COSTS AND AGENCY ORGANIZATION

Some of the causes of delay with its concomitant increase of costs have been set forth above. The existing state of the organization of many of the agencies is one chief reason for their delays. Their reorganization to correct this situation is thus essential and can be accomplished best and most expeditiously by the Executive. His constitutional responsibility to see that the laws are faithfully executed calls upon him to do so. The Executive, moreover, is less beset by the vested interests in bureaucracy that too often find support from members of the Congress. To do this, however, he must be empowered to act.

The first step consequently is, at least, to revive powers heretofore granted the President under the Reorganization Act of 1949, under which the power of the President to submit reorganization plans expired on June 1, 1959. A simple statute can do this. It would be better, however, in view of the bureaucratic pressures that are capable of being organized, as was evidenced by the defeat of President Truman's Plan No. 7 for the reorganization of the Interstate Commerce Commission, to require that the veto powers by the Congress over reorganization plans submitted by the President should require a majority in both Houses of Congress. The leadership of the President in these matters should be respected by the Congress unless he is palpably wrong.

Blueprints as to further reorganization of the various agencies cannot be submitted at this time. But certain ideas as to what the outlines of each reorganization should generally be can be suggested. These can best be set forth by a brief examination of some of the major regulatory agencies.

I. THE INTERSTATE COMMERCE COMMISSION

Among the agencies principally calling for reorganization is the Interstate Commerce Commission. It lacks positive direction because of the absence of the position of a chairman who is other than a presiding officer. The theory of a rotating chairman, elected annually by the membership, may assuage the ambitions of its membership, but it deprives the Commission of that leadership that it so sadly needs. The informed public generally knows the names of the heads of our Executive Departments and has some sense of the general policies that they advocate. But even the informed public within the railroad and trucking industries have no idea and care less who, for the time being, might be the Chairman of the Interstate Commerce Commission. The selection of the Chairman from among its membership is essential but it is equally essential that he be appointed to that office by the President and hold it at his pleasure. A chairman must evince an ability to manage the mechanism over which he presides so that delays and unnecessary bureaucratic procedures do not characterize its work. He must be able to obtain the respect and loyalty of his colleagues and, above all, take the lead in the formulation of the policies that the Commission should pursue. His powers should include the appointment of all personnel to the agency, save the heads of the prime Divisions or Bureaus where the assent of his colleagues can be required and also reserving to his colleagues certain excepted positions necessary to enable them to perform their individual tasks. He should have complete authority as to the internal organization of the agency, the divisions and bureaus into which it should be divided, and the complete responsibility, subject to the review of the Bureau of the Budget, for its budget. He should also be the spokesman for the agency before the Congress, the President, and the Executive Departments, although he naturally would advise with his colleagues on such matters as well as delegate to others matters that he believes can be better handled by them. He should not, however, restrict the free expression of views differing from his by his colleagues to the Congress, the President or the public.

Such a change would permit the centralization of responsibility for the operations of the agency in a manner whereby its operations can be far more easily evaluated by the Congress, the President and the public. Moreover, the position would then attach to itself a prestige equal to that of a Cabinet post, which it now plainly lacks. Nor would this change detract from the responsibilities and prestige of the other members for, by relieving them of their present multitudinous administrative duties, they could devote themselves, which they physically cannot do at the present time, to a personal consideration of the problems before them. It may be contended that such an arrangement would destroy the "independence" of the agency. This would not, however, be the fact, for the failure of the Chairman to retain the confidence and respect of his colleagues would create a situation justifying the President in replacing him by some other member competent to assume these responsibilities.

The membership of the Interstate Commerce Commission, eleven in number and the largest of any regulatory agency, gives ground for concern. Commissioners have been added to the Interstate Commerce Commission from time to time on the theory that their addition was necessary because of the increased work load of the Commission. The Commission was authorized to create panels of three or more members to dispose of cases before it and it has done so. However, the right to get a reconsideration of a panel decision by the full Commission has been so broad that reconsiderations or panel decisions are very frequently requested and too frequently granted. Reforms in this panel process of decision must be made so that rarely will the unwieldy number of eleven Commissioners be called on as a body to determine issues generally never more consequential than those finally disposed of by three judges in our Circuit Courts of Appeal.

Opinions of the Interstate Commerce Commission are presently in the poorest category of all administrative agency opinions. Their source is unknown and the practice has grown up of parsimony in discussing the applicable law in making a determination. Lengthy recitals of the contentions of the various parties are made as a prelude to a succinct conclusion devoid of real rationalization. This practice was inveighed against by a distinguished former member, Commissioner Aitcheson, but it has not been changed. The creation of an opinion writing section has been urged by the managerial consultants hired to survey the Commission. But opinion writing sections are not the answer even at their best as in the Securities and Exchange Commission. Individual Commissioners must be assigned the responsibility of expressing the conclusions of the Commission. They will, of course, need help and appropriate help in the nature of law clerks such as are now assigned to federal judges, rather than the present practice of temporarily assigning attorneys from the staff of a Bureau. Law clerks personally attached to a Commissioner will take pride in their chief's performance just as the law clerks seek now to perfect the work of their judges.

The individual commissioners are presently assigned administrative duties as supervisors of various Bureaus within the Commission. This is unnecessary and disruptive of the time of the Commissioners.

A major problem in the reorganization of the Interstate Commerce Commission, as in most other agencies, is the delegation of appropriate duties to persons below the Commission level. Some advance in this respect has been made by the organization of four employee boards to deal with a series of non-hearing cases from whose decisions an appeal can be made to the Commission. In hearing cases the decision can be carried to the full Commission level by exceptions directly from the hearing examiner's report or upon a request for reconsideration of a decision by a panel of Commissioners. Delegation of matters to a greater degree than this is admittedly made difficult by specific provisions of the Interstate Commerce Act which, more than any of the other basic statutes, defines the procedural requirements to be followed by the Commission. However, changes even in these procedural requirements could seemingly be effected by Presidential action under the Reorganization Act provided that no infringement is made upon the right of judicial review.

Whether a reorganization plan could make final the decisions by single Commissioners, hearing examiners, or employee boards in certain groups of cases might be debatable, but a reorganization plan could make them final subject to review akin to the selective review by certiorari now employed as the means by which the Supreme Court of the United States determines which decisions of the Circuit Courts of Appeal it wishes to review. A judicious use of such a scheme and an insistence on brief petitions for certiorari by counsel would cut down enormously the business demanding attention at the Commission level. The legality of such a plan under the concepts of due process is not truly questionable.

Even within the confines of the existing law marked improvement in the manner of handling the adjudicatory problems could be made. The single Commissioner technique is rarely, if ever, utilized. Replacing a panel of three by a single Commissioner would obviously conserve a portion of the time of two Commissioners.

Again, the problem of hearing examiners has been handled badly by the Interstate Commerce Commission. The Civil Service classification of some examiners are below those of examiners in the other major agencies. They are regularly assigned to particular Bureaus and are thus confined both in interest and outlook. They have been subjected to the indignity of time clock controls. They have neither secretaries nor other assistants to aid them and frequently are ill-housed. Their reports are also too frequently rewritten for no discernible purpose.

Other reorganizations of the functions of the Commission as well as the tightening and refining of its procedural rules can be effected without the need of a reorganization "plan", and would undoubtedly be effected by an energetic and competent chairman. Suggestions along these lines are contained in the Booz, Allen & Hamilton Report and in the valuable recent Report of the Special Advisory Committee to the Interstate Commerce Commission.

2. The Civil Aeronautics Board

The chief criticisms of the Civil Aeronautics Board center about (1) the inordinate delay in its disposition of proceedings, especially in route cases; (2) the fact that its procedures are such as to make extraordinarily complex the issues before it in various types of proceedings; (3) the intrusion of influences off the record that appear to be determinative of pending cases; (4) a failure to do forward planning of the type necessary to promote our air commerce to its desired level of efficiency.

The inordinate delay in its disposition of pending causes and the complexity of these proceedings arises out of the procedures it applies to them. Issues with regard to route extensions, new routes, and new services come before it for determination as a result of the filing of applications by carriers or would-be carriers. The disposition of these matters pursues no pattern or plan. The result is that issues with regard to the desirability of new routes and new services are commingled with issues as to what carriers should fly what routes, calling for a final judgement that has to be based on political, economic, sociological, business and aeronautical considerations. All the issues in such a proceeding are handled by the lengthy process of examining and cross-examining witnesses. This is a wasteful manner of establishing many of the basic facts.

Routes that in the public interest should be flown are capable of being determined without resort to proceedings of this character but as a result of staff studies carried on in a less formal manner. Evidence now being presented in a formal manner as to the needs of various communities for service, as to the community of interest between communties, as to the desirability for increased competition or the existence of sufficient adequate surface transportation, as to the type of service required and the potentiality of generating a sufficient quantum of air traffic, can all be determined beforehand by less legalistic and reasonably scientific methods, leaving for a "judicialized" hearing only the issue as to which of the competing carriers is to be selected for certification on any particular route. If necessary, hearings could be held on the staff study itself, which also could be of a less formal type. In any event, a procedure of this type would shorten these route proceedings immensely and would be likely to produce better route systems than those produced by the existing procedures.

A system somewhat along these lines was applied initially shortly after World War II in establishing our main international air routes and the resulting air route map has proved itself generally successful. True, following the hearings in the international route cases, modifications of the suggested routes were made by the Board and probably modifications of planned routes would result even from the limited hearings indicated above. But the difference between the suggested procedure and that now being employed is that the former employs the technique of planning whereas the latter starts with a map that is a *tabula rasa* and then permits a hodge-podge of routes to be drawn across its face by the applicants from which the Board finally selects a route pattern for reasons that it frequently cannot even articulate.

The problem of mergers should be handled in the same fashion. Mergers where desirable should follow and be considered within the framework of a planned and articulated transportation policy rather than being brought about by the happenstance of the financial difficulties of a carrier or because one carrier is willing to pay a higher price for a certificate than another carrier. Unfortunately, the Board has hamstrung itself so as to prevent this approach by permitting certificates freely given to a carrier by the Government to become a subject of barter in the market and thus be put on the auction block to be sold to the highest bidder for a price which the public is eventually bound to pay.

These suggested procedures would also affect the pattern of *ex parte* presentations. No objection could rightly be made to *ex parte* presentations at the informal stage, presentations that relate to the need or desirability of new air services. Only at the hearing stage where a choice has to be made as between competing applicants do *ex parte* presentations become truly harmful.

The institution of procedures of this type would seemingly require no legislative action. Furthermore, air carriers and air routes are now so plentiful that it might be desirable temporarily to freeze the situation and ponder over the road that has already been traveled in order to determine just what the next turning should be.

Ex parte presentations and the acceptance of unusual hospitalities have bedevilled the Board probably ever since its creation. They seem to have increased in recent years, although their extent is unknown except as some particular incident has brought them to light. Many of the airlines maintain substantial offices in Washington and have attached to them specialists under various titles whose function is primarily to maintain good relations between the airline and the members and staff of the Board. The control of this problem, which seems to have a greater incidence at the Civil Aeronautics Board, the

Federal Power Commission and the Federal Communications Commission—agencies with substantial favors to give out—is dealt with elsewhere in this report. But the Civil Aeronautics Board has a special problem arising out of the President's power over international and overseas routes, where no procedure for influencing the President's determination exists except *ex parte* presentations. There is probably no cure for this situation except the self-restraint, that has notably been lacking in the last two administrations, which the President should impose upon himself in limiting his intervention to considerations of foreign policy and national defense.

The lack of planning on the part of the Board stems from the burden of its adjudicatory work. Planning has been so neglected over the last few years that a staff, fit to be called a planning staff, can hardly any longer be said to exist. At every point major issues of policy remain undecided. Cases being dealt with now are already so obsolete that they even fail to raise these issues, so that policy fails to evolve as fast as it should from the adjudicatory process.

Reorganization to make planning possible is a matter of internal organization. The only need for a "plan" within the meaning of the Reorganization Act lies in further increasing the powers granted to the Chairman in 1950 to the full extent herein suggested for the Interstate Commerce Commission and to permit more flexibility in the delegation of those decisions which require no real ratiocination to hearing examiners or to bureau heads subject to a certiorari type of review by the Board. Among these delegable matters are, with rare exceptions, foreign air carrier permits, approval of air carrier agreements, interlocking arrangements and similar matters.

One internal adjustment should be made insofar as negotiations on international routes are concerned. The board as a whole should not participate in such negotiations, though it may well want to consider the nature of the proposals that could be made or that would be acceptable. The actual negotiations should be headed by one member assisted by a small staff and such representatives as the State Department might choose to take part in a particular negotiation. This would make both for a better negotiating atmosphere, the centralization of responsibility, and the conservation of the time of the other members of the Board.

3. The Securities and Exchange Commission

The problems of the Securities and Exchange Commission are relatively simple. Much of the delays that characterize its operation stem from the fact that it, more than any other agency, has been starved for appropriations. Even the recent increases have not restored the amounts formerly available. What has been responsible for this attitude other than pure ignorance as to the significance of its functions is difficult to fathom. But more than increasing its appropriations is necessary.

Much of the delay that attends the registration of securities could be eliminated by providing for simpler forms of registration and a simplified supervision of the process of registration with respect to seasoned securities, bonds and debentures with an A or B rating and preferred stocks that for a past period have shown an appropriate ratio of earnings to dividends payable on such stocks. In the case of seasoned securities of this nature, the issuer and underwriter should be relied on to furnish full and accurate statements of fact and deficiency letters could be substantially abolished. It could also relieve from registration requirements certain admittedly technical public offerings for which registration is now technically necessary. The necessity for maintaining a currently effective registration statement on convertible securities, options and warrants, when an adequate market exists for the basic securities and adequate information is available in annual financial reports or proxy statements, is an example of a situation where registration is unnecessary. The issuance of restricted options to groups of employees not too excessive in number is another such example. More of them can be found. Relieving the Commission and the industry of the necessity for acting on registration statements in such situations would clear the Commission's docket to some degree and relieve the industry of unnecessary costs.

The deficiency letter, a most valuable extra-legal development, has a real place with regard to the more promotional and speculative securities. There has grown up over the years a considerable tendency to indulge in lint-picking in these letters, resulting in delays and unnecessary costs. Another tendency has become noticeable due to the attitude of certain Commissioners shortly following World War II. This is to move away from the legislative standards of full disclosure to a judgement on the quality of the securities being registered. The history of state security regulation in this respect gives ample evidence of the undesirability of establishing a bureaucracy with powers of this nature. True, there is every temptation to move in this direction as one views as a whole the rapacity of promoters and underwriters and the unwillingness of a greedy and speculative public to try to understand the simplest facts of corporate finance. But control and supervision over the activities of the selling group and the marginal fringe of brokers and dealers making markets in these issues, can do more to dampen this type of financial piracy than the use of the registration powers for purposes for which it was not intended.

Similarly controls should be extended more widely as against so-called investment advisers, many of whom have morals not exceeding those of tipsters at the race track. Even our conservative newspapers carry horrendous advertisements as to the prowess of particular advisers and the aura that these advisers have engendered has led to imitation of their tactics by large and respectable brokerage houses. Here is a field that the Securities and Exchange Commission is beginning to plough and money made available for such a purpose will pay ample dividends in turning savings away from rank speculation to reasonable investment.

One serious feature of delay on the part of the Securities and Exchange Commission lies in the issuance of regulations and forms. Important regulations have been delayed for years. Some reason for this delay lies in the inherent complexities of the problems and the commendable practice of the Securities and Exchange Commission, so different from that of the Federal Aviation Agency, of affording opportunities to the industry to comment on proposed regulations. But an element of delay arises from the incapacity of the Commisioners themselves to grasp the essence of these problems and the significance of their resolution to the financial community. Because of the excellence of its staff and the inherent complexities of the problems, the Commission in a sense is the captive of its staff. It appears to be incapable at times of resolving differences within the staff and the resultant inaction makes for delay. The recent confirmed appointment of a career employee as a Commissioner may provide some remedy for this situation. But it points up the absolute necessity for having qualified individuals as members of the Commission.

Rapidity of decision in many matters is more important in the Securities and Exchange Commission than in most of the other regulatory agencies. The failure to get a decision or delay in making a decision is in itself defeat in many cases.

Delegation becomes essential. Too little of this characterizes the work of the Commission and, when it does exist, the line of delegation is not clear. Decisions, important decisions, are made by subordinates at fairly low levels and, because of time pressures of such importance to the business of financing, their decisions have to be accepted. On the other hand, in such simple matters as the acceleration of the effective date of registration statements, decision is not delegated and unnecessary time is consumed by the Commission in dealing with a problem that in nine out of ten cases is simple of solution.

The Securities and Exchange Commission has an opinion writing section whose quality is high, if not the highest among the agencies. Nevertheless, it should be abolished and individual Commissioners held individually responsible for the enunciation of the grounds upon which conclusions of the Commission are stated to rest. If the numerous speeches and articles of the various Commissioners are a test of their capacity for articulation, this should not be an impossible task.

The extension of the Commission's power of forcing appropriate disclosures with respect to securities in the over-the-counter-market— an extension long urged by the Commission—is a matter for legislative action. As an ideal it has basic merit, particularly with respect to categories of securities, such as bank and insurance stocks, which have traditionally refrained from listing on the stock exchanges. As a practical matter, certain restraining lines have to be drawn, perhaps tighter than those presently suggested by the Commission.

From the standpoint of the formal Presidential action needed with respect to the Securities and Exchange Commission, the only thing required is further strengthening the powers granted to the Chairman in 1950 to the full extent heretofore suggested for the Interstate Commerce Commission and the implementation of its powers to delegate adjudicatory matters to hearing examiners and employees.

4. The Federal Trade Commission

The problems of the Federal Trade Commission, apart from its overlapping jurisdiction with the Antitrust Division of the Department of Justice and the Food and Drug Administration, are purely internal. Here, as in the case of the Interstate Commerce Commission, the Civil Aeronautics Board and the Securities and Exchange Commission, the powers of the Chairman should be increased and the Commission's authority to delegate decision-making implemented by Presidential action under the Reorganization Act.

In 1954, a reorganization of the Commission, known as the Howrey reorganization, took place following the recommendations of the management consultants, Robert Heller and Associates. A major aspect of this reorganization resulted in a fractionalization of the handling of cases before the Commission and has proved to be a failure. This is not only the opinion of practitioners but of members of the staff of the Federal Trade Commission. In 1956, Subcommittee No. 1 on Regulatory Agencies and Commissions of the Select Committee on Small Business of the House of Representatives commented on this reorganization (at page 28) in the following terms:

"New and more paperwork was provided for, following reorganization which was recommended by Heller & Associates...

"Not only was the cost of operation of the FTC increased under this new reorganization by virtue of the increased paperwork as has been indicated, but the cost of operation of the FTC was also increased by virtue of the reorganization providing for new positions of high salaried people. Some examples of that are provided in the testimony before the subcommittee."

Not only were separate Bureaus of Investigation and Litigation set up but a system of "project attorneys" was introduced. The consequence of this is revealed by the following excerpt from a report on the operation of the Commission:

"For example, when the investigator submits the completed files, along with his recommendations, the case is reviewed by the Branch Manager and his assistant, by the project attorney, the Chief Project Attorney, by the Director of the Bureau of Investigation and his two assistants, by the trial attorney and by his superiors, the legal adviser, the Assistant Director, the Associate Director and the Director of the Bureau of Litigation before it is ever forwarded to the Commission for action.

"In the entire procedure the attached Status Report on cases shows that of all these reviewers, the project attorney takes the most time. Over 40 percent of the project attorney's cases are over one year old. Only 20 percent of the cases in field offices, where the actual investigation is conducted, are that old."

"If Litigation and Investigation were consolidated and the project attorneys were eliminated, the reviewing process would cut down to this: Investigator—Field Office Manager—Trial Attorney—Division Chief—Commission.

"At the same time, the project attorneys could be reassigned to the investigative or trial staffs. This would add thirty experienced attorneys to those staffs without any increase in payroll expense."

The trouble, however, lies even deeper than this. Because of the unfortunate early history of the Federal Trade Commission in the 1920's in which the courts bore down upon the loose procedures of the Commission, extensive records were made in false and deceptive practice cases before the Commission. This procedure has continued to this day with the consequence that protracted records and consequent delay characterizes the conduct of cases of this nature. If the advertiser of a drug states that "four out of five doctors" recommend it, to prove the falsity of such an allegation much massing of evidence ensues. This practice coupled with the fact that the Commission has no power to issue interlocutory cease and desist orders on the basis of a *prima facie* case, significantly emasculates the Commission's power to deal with the spate of deceptive advertising that floods our newspapers, our periodicals and our air waves. Whereas in the securities field puffing is kept to a minimum, *caveat emptor* is rampant in the sale of other products, even those bearing directly upon the public's health. It is not suggested that rules governing the sale of securities should be applicable to the sale of other products, but, if we are interested in minimizing false and deceptive advertising, some sanctions more effective than those presently possessed by the Federal Trade Commission must be fashioned. The interlocutory cease and desist order appealable to a court would be a first step. Absent such a remedy, years can elapse before any action is taken and then the only penalty is an order to cease and desist.

Other areas of the Commission's jurisdiction raise more complex issues both of facts and of law. Issues arising out of the concepts of monopoly and the stifling of competition are never simple. But they are not so immediate in their impact on the public as false and deceptive advertising. Also, the Robinson-Patman Act is an extremely poorly drafted statute. The scope of its operation has been muddled rather than clarified by court decisions. Nor has the Federal Trade Commission been able to fabricate clear standards out of its melange of generalities, qualified by proviso upon proviso. Remedial devices in this field can only be had from the Congress, which must make up its mind as to what this legislation is really intended to accomplish. Some better analyses of these problems could, however, be made by the Federal Trade Commission. The vigorous and imaginative leadership currently enjoyed by the Division of Trade Practice Conferences should be continued. This is a valuable supplement to the formal litigation activity of the Commission. The industry-wide consultation program can cure in a few weeks competitive ills that would require several years of formal litigation to cure.

A basic problem of the Federal Trade Commission relates to its overlapping jurisdiction in the antitrust field with the Department of

Justice, and in the food and drug field with the Food and Drug Administration. Over the years, it is beyond question that the Antitrust Division of the Department of Justice has been more effective than the Federal Trade Commission. The grant of statutory authority to the Department of Justice is broader, although there are a few areas where it cannot reach practices that the Federal Trade Commission can handle. The sanctions that the Antitrust Division can invoke are far more powerful than those possessed by the Federal Trade Commission with the result that consent decrees can be better and more easily achieved by the Department of Justice.

In the food and drug field the jurisdictional areas of the Federal Trade Commission and the Food and Drug Administration are again not identical, but they do overlap. The sanctions available to each agency are also different, with a measure of greater power residing in the Food and Drug Administration.

The overlap in both these areas calls for correction. A sensible arrangement would be to transfer the antitrust activities of the Federal Trade Commission (not including its Robinson-Patman Act jurisdiction) to the Department of Justice, and to the Federal Trade Commission the duties of the Food and Drug Administration now in the Department of Health, Education and Welfare, provided, of course, that each transferee can demonstrate its capacity to conduct a vigorous program in the discharge of these new responsibilities.

An overlap is also alleged to exist between the Federal Trade Commission and the Federal Communications Commission in the field of false and deceptive advertising over the radio waves. This, however, is unimportant. The Federal Trade Commission has the responsibility to deal with false and deceptive advertising whatever the means of communication employed. Whether as a consequence of indulging in such practices the status of a Federal Communications Commission licensee should be altered, is an appropriate consideration for the Federal Communications Commission.

An overlap also exists between the Federal Trade Commission and the Department of Agriculture with regard to unfair trade practices of persons in the meat packing industry. There is no reason why full jurisdiction over the meat packing industry in that respect should not be returned to the Federal Trade Commission.

One prime reason for close contact between the Executive and the Federal Trade Commission through its Chairman is the fact that the Federal Trade Commission simply cannot cover all the areas of trade in which unfair practices are brought to its attention. It must concentrate on specific fields such as cigarettes, toys, or textiles. This involves an issue of policy of which the Executive should not only be aware but which should be keyed to whatever over-all program is then the Administration's prime concern. The responsibility for concentration on a particular area should be the responsibility of the Executive and not the Federal Trade Commission.

5. THE FEDERAL COMMUNICATIONS COMMISSION

The Federal Communications Commission presents a somewhat extraordinary spectacle. Despite considerable technical excellence on the part of its staff, the Commission has drifted, vacillated and stalled in almost every major area. It seems incapable of policy planning, of disposing within a reasonable period of time the business before it, of fashioning procedures that are effective to deal with its problems. The available evidence indicates that it, more than any other agency, has been susceptible to *ex parte* presentations, and that it has been subservient, far too subservient, to the subcommittees on communications of the Congress and their members. A strong suspicion also exists that far too great an influence is exercised over the Commission by the networks.

The quality of its top personnel is, of course, primarily responsible for these defects. The members of the Commission do not appear to be overworked in the sense that the Commission's docket is bulging with cases calling for disposition. Nevertheless disposition lags. Only 32 cases, all dealing with broadcasting licenses, were decided by the Commission during fiscal 1959, other than cases dismissed or in which the examiner's report became final. Commission action following the examiner's report in 9 of these cases took from 6 to 12 months and in 10 cases from one year to two years. In broadcast license cases no criteria for decision have evolved. True, criteria of various different kinds are articulated but they are patently not the grounds motivating decision. No firm decisional policy has evolved from these case-by-case dispositions. Instead the anonymous opinion writers for the Commission pick from a collection of standards those that will support whatever decision the Commission chooses to make.

Observers of the procedures employed by the Commission agree that the issues litigated are unreal and a mass of useless evidence, expensive to prepare, is required to be adduced. The uselessness of much of this evidence derives from several causes. The first is that programming proposed by applicants is of high-sounding moral and ethical content in order to establish that their operation of a radio and television station would be in the "public interest". The actual programming bears no reasonable similitude to the programming proposed. The Commission knows this but ignores these differentiations at the time when renewal of licenses of the station is before them. Nevertheless, it continues with its Alice-in-Wonderland procedures. Also because of the varying standards that the Commission employs, a vast amount of unrealistic testimony is adduced to support each of these standards, incumbering the record with useless data.

On major policy matters, the Commission seems incapable of reaching conclusions. The UHF debacle has been plainly apparent for some 5 to 6 years. Nothing of any substantial consequence has yet been accomplished by the Commission to relieve the situation, although they are now purporting to make available additional VHF channels in one and two V-channel markets.

The procedures employed by the Commission in adjudicatory matters seem primarily at fault for these deficiencies. Leadership in the effort to solve problems seem too frequently to be left to commercial interests rather than taken by the Commission itself. No patent solution for this situation exists other than the incubation of vigor and courage in the Commission by giving it strong and competent leadership, and thereby evolving sensible procedures for the disposition of its business.

6. The Federal Power Commission

The Federal Power Commission without question represents the outstanding example in the federal government of the breakdown of the administrative process. The complexity of its problems is no answer to its more than patent failures. These failures relate primarily to the natural gas field, in the Commission's handling of its responsibilities with respect to the transmission and the production of natural gas. Enough has already been said about the delays in this field, so terribly costly to the public and so productive of unemployment in other basic industries.

These defects stem from attitudes, plainly evident on the record, of the unwillingness of the Commission to assume its responsibilities under the Natural Gas Act and its attitude, substantially contemptuous, of refusing in substance to obey the mandates of the Supreme Court of the United States and other federal courts.

The Commission has exhibited no inclination to use powers that it possesses to get abreast of its docket. Thousands of rate cases dealing with independent gas producers clutter its docket. Of this mass of cases Senator Paul H. Douglas of Illinois has pointed out that an exemption of producers of natural gas in interstate commerce for resale of less than 2 billion cubic feet per year would take 4,191 producers, whose total production of natural gas was only 9.26% of the total volume of gas purchased by interstate pipeline companies in 1953, out of the jurisdiction of the Commission. The portion of the total production accounted for by these small producers may have varied slightly since then but still remain insufficient to require them to be subjected to regulation in order to provide adequate protection to natural gas consumers against monopoly prices. Nevertheless, no effort has been made by the Commission to clear its docket of these inconsequential cases in order to come to grips with the relatively few remaining producers who do matter.

The recent action of the Commission on September 28, 1960 in promulgating area rates, whether ultimately legal or not, has come far too late to protect the consumer. The area prices there set forth substantially reject the rate base approach and the fixed area prices come close to approximately current maximum prices, which have more than doubled in the past five years. The Commission's past inaction and past disregard of the consumer interest has led the states to seek to force it to discharge its responsibilities. It is somewhat of a phenomenon in our national life for the state utility commissions to be ranged against a federal commission in an effort to protect consumers against monopolistic and excessive rates. That, however, is today's picture of federal regulations of the natural gas industry.

The transmission side of that industry presents the same picture. Delay after delay in certifications and the prescription of rates has cost the public millions of dollars.

An example of the inability of the Commission to control the disposition of its business is afforded by the following.

A substantial number of certificate filings made by independent producers and pipelines request nothing more than the authority to make increased or additional sales of natural gas to existing customers or to customers within the same areas. These applications do not pose complex problems, but the paperwork and the dozens of steps taken while processing those applications contribute materially to the backlog which presently confronts the Commission. Not only do these relatively minor cases stack up, but also their presence delays Commission action on the other vital matters before it.

At the specific request of the Commission, the Congress amended the Natural Gas Act in order to provide a simplified procedure to cope with problems in this category.   In 1942, in response to the Commission's urgent pleas, Congress enacted Section 7 (f) of the Natural Gas Act which provided, in the plainest terms, that the Commission should determine "the service area" for a regulated company, and "Within such service area as determined by the Commission a natural-gas company may enlarge or extend its facilities for the purpose of supplying increased market demands in such service area without further authorization."

Under the procedure presented by Section 7 (f), the Commission could readily eliminate thousands of unnecessary requests for authorizations.   For example, even though an independent producer holds a certificate to sell gas to a pipeline from certain leases, the subsequent acquisition of additional leases requires the independent producer to obtain further authorization in order to increase its sales to the same pipeline.   There is not a single instance in which this authority has ultimately been denied.   Nevertheless, the Commission has needlessly required the filing of separate applications.

Similarly, the Commission requires the complete gamut of pleadings and processing in order to enable an established producer to sell gas from a new well to an established pipeline at a price completely in line with prices theretofore certificated.

An identical problem is posed to a pipeline which wishes to meet the increased requirement of a distributor, even though no change in rate is involved.

It was to do away with these problems that Section 7 (f) was enacted.   Nevertheless, during the 18 years that provision has been in the statute, the Commission has not utilized it on a single occasion.

In early 1942, applications were filed by five pipelines for service area determinations.   Those applications have not been acted upon to this date.   Of course, the same is true of every subsequent application under Section 7 (f).

In 1944, the Commission attempted to justify its inaction on grounds that the wartime conditions required all available manpower for other purposes.   However, the Commission added: "This work on the determination of service areas should be pressed forward as vigorously as possible, as soon as the exigencies of war make it practicable for the Commission and the companies to conduct the necessary investigations and hearings.

Despite this and subsequent pious expressions, the Commission has literally done nothing to reduce the delays which have constantly increased. Instead, when Congress requested action the Commission merely addressed a letter on May 8, 1946 to all natural gas companies requesting their views regarding administration of the service area provision of the act. The Commission simply ignored the replies.

In January 1947, the Commission's staff prepared and submitted an extensive report to the Commission strongly recommending implementation of Section 7 (f), and recommended the preliminary action be taken forthwith "to effectuate the intent of Congress expressed in Section 7 (f)."

If the Commission has any legitimate reason for its 18 years of failure to implement Section 7 (f), it has not given any expression thereto. Moreover, any possible criticism of the service area procedure provided by Congress at the Commission's request could readily be handled by the attachment of suitable conditions to service area determinations.

Other instances of ineffective administration are legion. Indeed, the dissatisfaction with the work of the Commission has gone so far that there is a large measure of agreement on separating from the Commission its entire jurisdiction over natural gas and creating a new commission to handle these problems exclusively.

It is probably unnecessary to go this far. However, certain amendments to the Natural Gas Act are essential. The Commission might well be increased to seven members so as to permit it to sit in two panels of three with final decision in each panel, so as to help it clear up its enormous back log. But primarily leadership and power must be given to its Chairman and qualified and dedicated members with the consumer interest at heart must be called into service to correct what has developed into the most dismal failure in our time of the administrative process.

7. THE NATIONAL LABOR RELATIONS BOARD

When the National Labor Relations Act (Wagner Act) was enacted in 1935, its administration was vested in a National Labor Relations Board made up of three members. The Board appointed its own General Counsel, and the appointment and direction of the staff, both in Washington and in Regional offices, were vested in the Board. The Board handled all aspects of both unfair labor practices and questions of representation. Thus, the same agency determined what cases to prosecute, conducted the prosecution, and rendered the decision. This pattern of organization was the same as that of other, older administrative agencies like the Interstate Commerce Commission and the Federal Trade Commission. In practice, the prosecuting and adjudicating functions were separated by internal divisions in the staff in a manner fully consistent with the requirements of the Administrative Procedure Act, which was enacted in 1946. Indeed, only marginal changes in the Board's procedures had been required by the Administrative Procedure Act.

In 1947, the Labor Management Relations Act (Taft-Hartley Act) was enacted. This Act, amending the Wagner Act, made a further separation between the prosecution and adjudicatory functions of the Board. It created the office of the General Counsel, to be filled by the President for a term of four years with the advice and consent of the Senate. The General Counsel was given the power to issue or withhold complaints and the entire legal staff, except legal assistants, appointed to assist Board Members prepare their decisions, was placed under his supervision. He also has general supervision of the Regional offices. The Board, expanded to five members, was continued as an administrative agency with powers to adjudicate upon complaints of unfair labor practices and with responsibility for handling all aspects of questions of representations, including the actual conduct of elections.

Since 1947 there have been no further statutory changes affecting the basic administrative pattern of the National Labor Relations Act.

There are, of course, various explanations as to why the administrative structure was changed in the foregoing manner in the Taft-Hartley Act. An Advisory Panel on Labor Management Relations Law to the Senate Committee on Labor and Public Welfare On The Organization And Procedures Of The National Labor Relations Board, established pursuant to a 1959 Senate Resolution, has stated with respect to the reasons for the change as follows in its January 1960 Report:

"In practice the prosecuting and adjudicating functions were separated by internal divisions in the staff. The functions merged only in the small percentages of cases in which the Board members themselves decided whether a complaint should issue, but regardless of whether this was intrinsically fair the emotional character of labor-management discussions, the controversies attendant upon the growth of strong unions and the spread of collective bargaining, and the suspicion of administrative bias, all lent color to the criticism that one body was acting as prosecutor, judge, and jury."

Others tend to the view that the forces which led to the enactment of the substantive provisions of the Taft-Hartley Act desired that a dominant voice in its administration should be given to a General Counsel subject to fresh confirmation by the Senate rather than to a Board which had been administering the statute prior to those amendments which were widely considered to be less than favorable to organized labor.

In any event, "the difficulty of administering one statute through two heads", to use the phrase of the Senate Committee's Advisory Panel, soon became apparent. In its January 1960 Report the Advisory Panel listed five "troublesome problems" which had engendered "controversies sufficiently bitter to erupt into public view":

(1) There were differences between the General Counsel and the Board concerning the exercise or declination of jurisdiction in unfair labor practices, the General Counsel taking the view that he alone had power to say when jurisdiction should be assumed, and the Board asserting the same power.

(2) There were disputes concerning the enforcement and review of National Labor Relations Board orders, both as to who had responsibility for determining whether there was sufficient compliance with the Board's order, and in those cases where the General Counsel demurred at defending orders issued by the Board over his objection or upon a rationale which he regarded as unsound.

(3) There were differences which affected the interrelationship between questions of representation and unfair labor practice cases.

(4) There was "argument and dissension" concerning the appointment and control of staff in Regional offices.

(5) There were differences in connection with the General Counsel's refusal to issue complaints. "Although the Board might adopt one rule of law or policy, the General Counsel could easily thwart the Board's decisions by declining to issue a complaint based upon the Board's philosophy."

Summing up, the Advisory Panel concluded that "there is little doubt that the controversies between the General Counsel and the Board have hampered the enforcement of the National Labor Board Act." These differences "are certain to continue so long as the present arrangement persists with the degree of intensity varying according to the personalities of individual officials." Accordingly, the Advisory Panel, which was composed of the most prominent authorities in the labor law field in the country, unanimously recommended "abandonment of the present hybrid compromise."

As the Senate Committee's Advisory Panel observed, revision of the present "two-head" system may take either of two forms: The first, which was recommended by President Truman in a plan of reorganization defeated in the Congress in 1950, is to restore the pattern of organization of administrative agencies such as the Federal Trade Commission, relying upon the Administrative Procedure Act to guarantee sufficient separation between the prosecuting and adjudicating functions. In fact, this would mean a return to the administrative pattern before the Taft-Hartley Act, since the Labor Board had functioned in compliance with the Administrative Procedure Act before 1947. Alternatively, those functions now performed by the Board other than the adjudication of unfair labor practice cases, could be transferred to the General Counsel and his title changed to that of "Administrator". This would mean that he would secure complete control over all personnel, other than the Board and its legal assistants, and would acquire jurisdiction over representation cases in addition to retaining the General Counsel's present complete control over the issuance of complaints in unfair labor practice cases. This second solution represents the view of the Advisory Panel.

In its report the Advisory Panel considered the advantages and disadvantages of each of these alternative solutions before deciding to recommend the second. It admitted frankly that a single administrative agency has the advantage of having "central direction of the manifold lines of activity which are required to implement a broad legislative policy," pointing out that such implementation involves not merely the adjudication of cases but also "the informal adjustment of charges, the selection and timing of cases for prosecution, decisions concerning the relative emphasis to be placed upon different aspects of the statute, the balance to be achieved between negotiated settlements and rigorous prosecution, and the presentation of cases in the courts." It emphasized that the lack of centralized direction of all phases of investigation, prosecution, adjudication and appellate litigation "would seriously hamper the development of programs under new social or economic legislation which are expressed in terms sufficiently general to leave scope for administrative discretion and the evolution of new legal concepts."

Despite these powerful arguments, the Panel nevertheless cited developments which in its view have reduced the occasion for unified control in the administration of the National Labor Board Act. The first such development cited by the panel was since "most of the basic policies and legal concepts have now been established", administration now requires "emphasis on the enforcement of existing rules rather than the creation of new programs or principles." But in the very month (January 1960) in which the Advisory Panel talked about the crystallization of rules and indicated that what was necessary was emphasis on the enforcement of them, the General Counsel of the National Labor Relations Board stated in a speech at the University of Minnesota, that " ... on the substantive side of the law, we are today indeed in a period of transition, readjustment, and adaptation." And earlier, in November 1959 in addresses at San Francisco and in New York, he discussed in detail "the puzzling provisos" in the 1959 changes in the National Labor Act, relating to the barring of organizational picketing, secondary boycotts, the resolution of the Federal-State jurisdictional problem, the special provision relating to construction contracts, and other difficult areas of interpretation and administration caused by the 1959 substantive amendments to the Labor law. Nor were the 1959 Amendments the only area of uncertainties and creative administration. As the General Counsel stated in his San Francisco speech:

"... the General Counsel must, by the very nature of his position, make the initial interpretations of the law ... Although most cases— and here I am speaking of those arising under the old law—are governed by established legal precedents, these are always a small but significant number of cases which present novel or difficult questions of law or policy. *These are the cases, which are significant in the administration of the Act, and which give it full content and meaning.* After twelve years the meaning of the 1947 amendments in critical areas is still being litigated ... "

The Advisory Panel also advanced what may have been a persuasive reason for its failure to support the first alternative solution to the present problem. It stated that "any return to the original set-up would revive old fears, justified or unjustified, of a one-sided tribunal serving as both prosecutor and judge."

The Advisory Panel's conclusions on this major issue follow generally the lines of the survey of the NLRB made by McKinsey and Company, Inc., Managerial Consultants, at the request of the Bureau of the Budget. Neither the conclusions of the Advisory Panel or the managerial consultants are too persuasive. Friction between the General Counsel and the Board, so continuingly serious, is not likely to be significantly reduced. Their disparate positions are such that rivalry between them is inevitable. Nor can a separation be made between them with reference to the handling of unfair labor practice cases and representation cases since too frequently one controversy will involve both issues. A return to the earlier system, a conclusion reached in an excellent study by the Bureau of the Budget itself in 1958, seems preferable to the Advisory Panel's solution, although the latter would bring about improvements over what presently exists.

Inordinate delay and docket congestions of the type that characterizes the other major regulatory agencies is not the pattern of the business before the National Labor Relations Board. Figures covering fiscal year 1958 disclose that of the unfair labor practice cases filed, 88% are disposed of in the field in an average of 51 days by withdrawal, dismissal or settlement. Of the remaining 12%, in which formal complaints are issued, only 5.6% call for formal Board action. The average time for disposition from initiation of the complaint to final disposition, however, is too long being somewhat under 500 days. The record in representation cases is better. Although notices of hearing are issued in 46% of these cases, and 23% go to the Board after hearing, 18% of these are disposed of on the average by the short form proceeding within 80 days from the issuance of the notice of hearing and the balance of long form proceedings average some 120 days for final disposition.

Here again giving more effective finality to the examiner's finding is the answer. A suggestion to this effect is now pending before the Board in the form of certain recommended rules of practice drafted by a committee headed by Board Member Jenkins. But more finality can be achieved by a Presidential reorganization plan than by these proposals.

8. Other Regulatory Agencies

A particularistic analysis of other regulatory agencies is not included herein. Their problems are not generally like those of the agencies discussed above. The Federal Maritime Board, for example, raises different organizational problems due to the executive responsibilities it possesses and the existence of a Maritime Administrator responsible to the Secretary of Commerce. But in its quasi-judicial aspects it suffers from a lack of settled, public procedures and standards of decision thus resulting in the exercise frequently of arbitrary powers by the staff. It places too much emphasis on bureaucratic details to the disregard of matters of large public importance. A fog of secrecy also surrounds many actions of the Board and no articulate standards seem to have developed with respect to *ex parte* presentations. Each agency, however, requires separate consideration and individual remedial action.

9. ACTION IMMEDIATELY DESIRABLE

These steps should now be taken:

(1) Reorganization plans should be prepared covering the agencies named above, strengthening the position of the Chairmen, having them designated in all instances by the President and holding the office of Chairman at the pleasure of the President. These plans should also include provisions permitting delegation of the decision making powers to subordinate officials, such as hearing examiners or employee boards, subject only to a limited administrative review by the agency itself. No effort should be made to affect the existing scope of judicial review.

(2) Budgetary needs should be carefully surveyed so that the work of the agencies should not be hampered by a false sense of economy.

(3) Further reorganization plans of a more extensive nature should be prepared dealing with the individual necessities of the agencies. Those in the worst situation such as the Federal Power Commission, the Federal Communications Commission, the Interstate Commerce Commission and the Civil Aeronautics Board, should be given preference. The responsibility for the preparation of these plans should be centered in the Office of the President. Enough formal studies and material now exists to enable the fashioning of these plans.

B. PERSONNEL

The prime key to the improvement of the administrative process is the selection of qualified personnel. Good men can make poor laws workable; poor men will wreck havoc with good laws.

As long as the selection of men for key administrative posts is based upon political reward rather than competency, little else that is done will matter. Thus, the real issues are two: (1) are these posts sufficiently attractive to draw good men, and (2) how can these men be found?

Good men are primarily attracted by the challenge inherent in a job. Salary is a secondary consideration, provided only that it is high enough to enable them to meet reasonable standards of living comparable to their positions in the society. Our universities have known and, indeed, traded on these facts. Tenure is another consideration of more importance than salary, for with tenure goes independence and the opportunity for long-range planning.

Basic challenges have been missing in the last decade. Good men cannot be attracted to agencies if they see that the colleagues with whom they are called upon to work, the staffs that they must utilize, are not measurable by standards they believe to be appropriate. Such a condition implies a lack of concern or a lack of understanding of the regulatory process by the President, either or both of which are destructive of the very thing that could hold an appeal. The appeal of a job can also be destroyed if the President, through design or neglect, permits his prejudices in behalf of political associates or friends to dictate the deposition of individual items of business. No truly good man can submit to such interference. Finally, the job's relationship to the general program of the Administration must be clear and that clarity of relationship with the help of the President constantly maintained. These are the essential ingredients of the concept of challenge. They are also essential lures for the enlistment of talent.

Compensation is a consideration. Present salaries for top administrative personnel are in the neighborhood of $20,000 per year. This is a reasonable salary for the present level of the cost of living. Increasing it by $2500 or even $5000 would not appreciably affect the situation. But there are two things that could make these positions more attractive at a very reasonable cost. The first is the grant of a moderate entertainment allowance to the administrator. Like an ambassador he needs to maintain a certain prestige with the industry. He should be able to entertain rather than be required to suffer entertainment. At conferences, which he not infrequently is required to call, luncheon breaks should provide something better than service from a government cafeteria. The second matter is an adequate retirement allowance. For unexplained reasons the retirement allowance for executive employees is considerably less than the allowances available to legislators. As an alleged servant of the Congress, the independent Commissioner or his counterpart could be enfolded within the legislative scheme. This fringe benefit could well make a difference.

Chairmen, especially if their powers are enhanced, should be compensated on a better basis than their colleagues for they have more to do. The present difference rarely runs over $500 a year, a sum which is neither sufficient to be compensatory nor to make for prestige.

Tenure is of importance. A term of five or seven years is too short. If the appointee is a lawyer or in business, conflict of interest laws require him to sever all his past connections. To give up a practice patiently accumulated over the years is not easy, for it may well become necessary to spend years again in re-establishing it. To eliminate oneself from a place in the ascending ladder of a business organization

raises similar problems. Moreover, longer tenures would mean opportunities for longer-scale planning, freedom from worry as to re-
appointment, and generally the concept of devotion to a career rather
than that of a stepping stone to further political or professional advancement. Turnover would probably be reduced as is true of the
members of the Federal Reserve Board whose tenures are fourteen
years. Expertise would have a better chance to develop and the sense
of security would inculcate the spirit of independence. Life tenure
is, perhaps, too dangerous in these areas of dynamic activity but certainly a ten year term is not too much to suggest .

Given competent appointments to deal with real challenges which
can be made to exist, the recruitment of a competent staff is not difficult. Great universities have never had their difficulties on this score
and great administrative agencies could offer a similar challenge. Both
should possess essentially the same opportunity of objectivity and the
same urge to search for answers to pressing problems, with the balance,
so far as the practically minded man is concerned, in favor of the
latter. But the key to staff competence can only be found through
the existence of inspiration and competency at the top level.

C. ETHICAL CONDUCT AND INDUSTRY ORIENTATION

Conflicts of interest appear not to be a serious problem in the regulatory agencies. As the Association of the Bar of the City of New
York in its recent study of this general problem entitled "Conflict of
Interest and the Federal Service", remarked: "The substantive regulations of many agencies show forth as relatively integrated, more
modern [than the conflict of interest statutes], better drafted and, most
important, as relevant expressions of public policy". The real problem
centers about *ex parte* presentations.

The definition of what constitutes an undesirable *ex parte* presentation is not easy. As difficult is the definition of the circumstances under
which such presentations can be appropriately made and those circumstances under which the making of substantially the same presentation is wrongful. The source of the presentation also bears on the
factors as to whether it is wrongful or not. Again, there is the question
of what sanctions should be employed against them and how to
handle oral *ex parte* presentations as to which disputes will arise as
to the fact, the manner and the nature of their utterance. Finally,
there is the question of what sanctions should be employed to eradicate
them.

Both houses of the Congress have recently been struggling with these problems and considerable refinement of the ways in which to define and deal with those that are wrongful has taken place. Further advances can be expected to be made as the next Congress is certain to return to the problem.

The issue here considered is whether action of any kind should be taken by the Executive with respect to this problem. Executive action would have the virtue of defining with some degree of particularity what conduct would constitute grounds for removal from the public service by the President or other persons empowered to remove public servants for cause. It would also presumably furnish a criterion for the action of professional associations, such as bar associations or boards of accountancy, in disciplining their members. It would not, however, reach the worst source of these presentations, namely the regulated industries themselves except insofar as their presentations might be made by persons in the organized professions. It would also not extend to Congressmen and Senators.

The only way in which these latter categories could be reached would be by the legislative creation of criminal sanctions. The objections to doing so lie in the difficulty of defining the crime and the difficulty of convicting guilty offenders. The latter is probably a difficulty but not a valid objection to action. Convictions under our anti-lobbying statutes are rare but they nevertheless have been useful in reducing the blatant lobbying practices that preceded their enactment.

Presidential action by way of executive order in this field appears desirable even though it is necessarily limited in its impact. But such an executive order should be couched in general terms. It should eschew any effort to enter into details such as to seek to define when a proceeding becomes a proceeding on the record—a question now pending before the Civil Aeronautics Board and one which is likely to be carried to the courts. It should not seek to devise mechanisms for the manner in which allegedly oral *ex parte* presentations are to be made of record or circulated among interested parties who in many proceedings may number a hundred or more. Reputations can easily be irreparably damaged by well-intentioned but misguided or erroneous action.

The virtue of proscriptions generally worded is that they can and will be expounded in later proceedings and in the light of concrete situations. This is a field where circumstances will vary so markedly that we shall need to build slowly, brick by brick and case by case.

But the President should initiate that process by laying the foundations for such a development through executive action.

Industry orientation of agency members is a common criticism, frequently expressed in terms that the regulatees have become the regulators. Of course, if ths type of orientation characterizes an individual prior to his appointment, there is little that can be done about it. But the real problem relates to those who are originally oriented towards the public interest but who gradually and honestly begin to view that interest in terms of private interest. This is particularly likely to occur in agencies which in addition to their regulatory functions have promotional functions. It was manifested in the innate reaction of the Civil Aeronautics Board to the non-scheduled airlines and to the newer all-cargo air carriers. The Civil Aeronautics Board to date has not considered the provision of subsidy to these all-cargo air carriers. This is not a plea that it should urge the provision of such subsidy, but some rationalization for the grant of subsidy to local service carriers and its denial to the all-cargo air carriers should be made, since there is an obvious national interest in expanding the development of this branch of our transportation system. The Interstate Commerce Commission has frequently been characterized as railroad-minded, the Federal Communications Commission as dominated by the networks, while the actions of the Federal Power Commission speak for themselves.

This tendency toward industry orientation is subtle and difficult to deal with. It arises primarily from the fact that of necessity contacts with the industry are frequent and generally productive of intelligent ideas. Contacts with the public, however, are rare and generally unproductive of anything except complaint. For example, the public that our security legislation is designed to protect is the "investor", but the investor rarely appears and when he does he is too rarely an investor and too frequently a speculator who deserves exactly what happened to him.

Irrespective of the absence of social contacts and the acceptance of undue hospitality, it is the daily machine-gun-like impact on both agency and its staff of industry representation that makes for industry orientation on the part of many honest and capable agency members as well as agency staffs. A device, employed in some agencies, is some protection against this tendency. This is the device of the public counsel, the effectiveness of whose function is in almost direct relationship to his capacity to irritate the agency members. It should be encouraged, however, and the public counsel, in those cases where he has intervened, should be granted the right of seeking review from the decisions of trial examiners to the agency itself on terms accorded to the parties themselves, although a right to seek judicial review of decisions that have achieved finality should naturally be denied him since the public interest has presumably by that time coagulated in the agency's decision.

D. ADMINISTRATIVE PROCEDURE

Much work has been done in the field of improving administrative procedures since the passage of the Administrative Procedure Act of 1946. These improvements were preceded by intensive research and study. The chief contributors in this field have been organizations such as the Hoover Commission and various bar associations, scholars and individual practitioners. Much of the thinking by now has been fairly well crystallized and should soon be ready for formulation into legislation and administrative rules of practice and procedure. The difficulty presently is the absence of continuing effort and the lack of a point where such effort can be focalized so that action will ensue.

In 1953, the President sent out a call for a conference on the subject of administrative procedure which was attended by representatives of the various federal regulatory agencies, and distinguished members from the bench, the bar and the universities. A report was made by this conference in 1955 containing a series of important recommendations to the agencies as well as the Judicial Conference of the United States. With the close of the conference, there was no follow-up. However, one recommendation of the conference suggested that it, or something similar to it, be placed on a permanent basis and this recommendation was endorsed by the American and Federal Bar Associations as well as the Judicial Conference of the United States. On August 29, 1960, the President requested Judge Prettyman of the Court of Appeals for the District of Columbia Circuit to undertake the preliminary work of organizing such a conference. Judge Prettyman in turn appointed a committee of 14 members and has ready a preliminary draft of by-laws for such an organization.

This work should be encouraged and Judge Prettyman, whose knowledge of and devotion to the subject is well-known, should be requested to continue his efforts. Much can come from this effort, including not merely revisions in our administrative procedures but also the making of our regulatory agencies into a system just as the Judicial Conference of the United States has made a system of what were once isolated and individual federal courts. But for a conference of this type to be effective it is essential that a permanent secretariat be established, which can follow the work of various committees, break out issues and problems that require exploration and research, arrange for appropriate publications, and act as liaison agent between the conference, the Congress and the government generally.

The work and functions now lodged in the Office of Administrative Procedure in the Department of Justice should be transferred to this secretariat for the statistics can there be refined and reworked so as to make them significant to the operations of the conference. A second function now vested in the Civil Service Commission, that of the qualification and grading of hearing examiners, could also be transferred to this secretariat. The situation presently is admittedly a not too happy one. The Civil Service Commission is not fundamentally organized to handle this problem. The extremely important goals of maintaining the independence and integrity of the hearing examiners and of evolving a corps of highly qualified examiners can better be achieved through an arrangement of this character rather than leaving these problems to the Civil Service Commission.

Experiments in the flexibility of handling this corps and promoting a better use of examiners through an effort to make them at least partly fungible could be carried on by the secretariat and could make for uniformity and improvement in administrative procedures through the interchange of experience and knowledge. The secretariat could also be a central spot for the recruitment of lawyers for the government, particularly for the regulatory agencies.

The concept of an Administrative Conference of the United States promises more to the improvement of administrative procedures and practices and to the systematization of the federal regulatory agencies than anything presently on the horizon. It could achieve all that the concept of the Office of Administrative Procedure envisaged by the Hoover Commission and endorsed by the American Bar Association hoped to accomplish, and can do so at a lesser cost and without the danger of treading on the toes of any of the agencies.

E. The Coordination of Agency Policy

Coordination of agency policy is meaningless in the absence of the internal development of policy by the individual agencies. The lack of such development in recent years has been commented upon and, in previous sections methods have been suggested as how that deficiency

could be cured, namely the evolution of new procedures, the strengthening of planning divisions and the relief of agency members themselves from the multitudinous and frequently minor duties that they
are required to perform.

In various areas, however, agency policies must be coordinated
and welded into an integrated whole. Certain areas such as transportation, communication and energy are obvious areas where such
coordination is essential. It has not infrequently been suggested
that something akin to a Ministry or Department of Transportation
with cabinet rank should be created. Many other countries have
such departments and they are operated with considerable success.
There are, however, striking differences between the situation in these
countries and that which prevails in the United States. The area and
scope of the problems differ decisively. No other nation possesses
the vast network of surface transportation, both common carrier and
private, that stretches over this country; nor does any nation possess
the air route mileage or the vast fleet of planes maintained and operated by the people of the United States. But far more significant than
this is the fact that the common carrier systems of these nations, with
the exception of shipping, are generally owned and operated by their
governments. We, on the other hand, have developed privately owned
common carrier systems and have relied on the forces of competition
to maintain these systems at their maximum efficiency. Our success in
this approach has been generally recognized and, as a nation, we would
be loathe to abandon it. The result is that in the transportation field
our problems of controlling excessive competition, of restraining monopolistic practices, of promoting new forms of competition, do not
raise controversies capable of internal settlement within the framework of a governmental bureaucracy. They present instead conflicts
between various carriers interests, between carriers and the public,
and between carriers and the government. Beginning in 1887, we
erected tribunals or administrative commissions to resolve these
various conflicts and, because of the emergence decade after decade
of new means of transportation, tribunals were created to deal with
problems that at the time seemed capable of being handled most
efficiently by specialists in particular fields. We are scarcely ready
to reverse an approach that can over the years be regarded as having
been successful simply because of the rising need for over-all planning
and coordination.

Nevertheless, plans and blueprints for mechanisms such as a Department of Transportation have been in existence for years and new ones

are being devised. None have as yet received substantial Congressional or Executive support. The blueprints, even the best of them, are unrealistic, beautiful in design but lacking in the appreciation of those earthy factors that are embedded in our regulatory transportation structure. Most of them entail the concept of some person in the nature of a czar sitting astride the whole transportation structure and exercising through subordinate bodies many of the functions now vested in the regulatory agencies. Others conceive of splitting away the adjudicatory functions but consolidating other functions in an executive department. It may be that we can eventually attain some such goal but the means of reaching it or an equally satisfactory goal must still be developed.

The history of the evolution of the War Production Board is of interest in this respect. The Board, although its machinery was not free from defects, successfully mobilized the greater part of our national productive plant for war purposes. We have had nothing in peace time that had as broad powers and as wide an area of concern as the War Production Board. It did not, however, spring Minerva-like from the brain of a Jove. Its evolution was painful and personal and institutional tragedies marked its coming into being. It had numerous antecedents such as the Office of Production Management, the Supply Priorities and Allocation Board, and the National Defense Advisory Council, but eventually building upon the failures of these mechanisms, the War Production Board was brought into being and successfully survived the tremendous pressures generated by the demands of war. Similarly, the experiences of the Air Coordinating Committee laid the ground work for the Federal Aviation Act of 1958, a distinctly empiric piece of legislation.

If we would build towards the goal of coordinating our transportation system and its problems, we should do this carefully and on the basis of accumulating experience not merely as to problems but as to mechanisms to deal with these problems. A beginning along this line was made in 1953 by the creation in the Department of Commerce of an Undersecretary of Transportation. Although valuable work has been done in this office, that mechanism is probably not sufficient for the task. The reason is not necessarily the men who hold that office. It is the nature of the office itself. An office capable of doing such a task cannot be subordinate to the Secretary of Commerce, for its responsibilities are vaster and more important than all the other functions vested in the Department of Commerce. An arrangement of this nature makes achievement of these goals impossible. Such subordination destroys the very element of prestige necessary if leadership in this area is to evolve. It removes the fashioning of transportation policy one and even two steps from the President and, in so doing, permits the intrusion into that field of personages of lesser consequence weakening the sense of an authoritative approach to the problem as a whole.

The evolution of a national transportation policy must have a close and intimate relationship to the President. To do so by the creation of an executive department, however, means the imposition of presently undefined executive duties in the head of that department. These duties could probably be more defined at a later date in the light of experience and then vested without too much controversy in an appropriate governmental unit. Meanwhile, development of the coordinating function could be placed in the Executive Office of the President. It should not be vested in a White House assistant because such coordinating activity needs a protection from trivia, from personality conflicts and even from politics, as well as the objectivity of approach that can be given the coordinating authority by vesting it in an office already constituted to perform staff and not personal functions for the President. The office would need no regulatory powers. It does need the constant personal support of the President and through him the President's Cabinet and the Bureau of the Budget. Given these, a coordination of policy can be effected by such an office among the various regulatory agencies, implemented where necessary by executive order. And, as experience demonstrates, coordination and consolidation of functions among them can be effected by the wise use of the President's power under the Reorganization Act.

A tentative program of what could be accomplished through such an office by way of immediate objectives and longer range objectives follows. A minimum of legislation is required for the immediate objectives. The longer range objectives may call for revision of policies hitherto established by Congress and fundamental legislative changes.

A. The achievement of a program for the amelioration of interurban public transportation, including the establishment of metropolitian transit commissions with federal aid in the form of matching guaranteed loans for the acquisition and improvement of facilities and equipment under sound engineering, operating, and financing plans.

B. Formulation of policies to coordinate Federal highway aid programs with approved metropolitan transit plans, so as to promote the economic soundness and efficiency of metropolitan public transportation systems as a whole, with emphasis on the avoidance of traffic congestion and the decline of public transportation.

C. Rationalization of government transport needs, including military transportation, so as not to compete with the commercial systems.

D. Evolution of Federal, State and local tax policies to assure that tax relief to railroads is compensated for in improved service.

E. Formulation of policies, through the establishment of joint service boards, to encourage through-routing and joint-service among and between all forms of freight transportation, with simplification of billing and freight charges.

F. Formulation of policies relating to approval of consolidations and unification of carriers, both within and between different modes of transportation, which give greater weight to reduction of transportation costs and improvement of service.

G. Formulation of policies with respect to the approval of abandonment of railroad routes or services, and the curtailment of service, to assure that the needs of the affected traffic are adequately served by other transportation.

H. Establishment of a coordinated statistical gathering, processing, and analytical service to provide reliable domestic transportation data for policy formulation and rate regulation. Such a service does not now exist.

I. Review and revision of the policies of the Army Corps of Engineers with respect to river and harbor maintenance and improvement to discourage the uneconomic expansion of outport facilities.

J. Re-examination of Merchant Marine subsidy policies to reduce uneconomic competition on over-expanded trade routes in foreign commerce.

Among the longer range objectives are the following:

A. Revision of Section 4 of Part I of the Interstate Commerce Act to modify or abolish the authority of the Commission to grant railroads relief against water carrier competition.

B. Modification of the statutory powers of the Interstate Commerce Commission and the Civil Aeronautics Board in the matter of granting certificates of convenience and necessity, to require as the basis for granting or withholding certificates and permits, greater reliance upon a satistical showing of operating costs, quality of service, and ability of efficient carriers to expand, rather than mere customer support, too often artifically inspired.

C. Steps to establish cost of service, as the principal factor for determining the reasonableness of transportation rates.

D. Formulation of a policy for regulating the entry of private carriers into the field of domestic surface transportation, and revision of the present statutory exemptions.

E. Formulations of a program of financial aid to distressed railroads to take the place of Chapter 19 of the Interstate Commerce Act (49 U. S. C. 1231) with revision to ensure that the borrower will have a sound capital structure, and that improvements in equipment and service will result from the financial aid.

F. A reconsideration of the field of user charges for federal facilities, particularly as regards air carriers, trucks and inland waterways.

G. Foreign carrier competition both by sea and by air and the evolution of policies as to the position that American carriers should rightly occupy in this field.

The equivalent of cabinet meetings at a sub-cabinet level of the more important agency chairmen would contribute to the development of a sense of cohesion among the agencies. The office in turn at stated periods would be called upon to report progress or the lack of it to the President and his Cabinet.

Similar approaches can be made by the creation of similar offices for the areas of communications and energy. In communications the lack of coordination in both the international and national field is apparent. Neither the State Department nor the Office of Civil and Defense Mobilization is capable of affording the necessary leadership. Their other activities are too varied to permit communication to reach the high level of concern that it must reach. Indeed, only this month a staff report prepared for the Senate Committee on Aeronautical and Space Services made as one of its prime recommendations: "The most careful and comprehensive study should be undertaken by the Executive Branch without delay to examine elements of public policy concerned with communications, specifically as related to (a) the identification of central Federal authority for communication policy ... " Time, tide, and space wait for no man and it may be later than one thinks.

It is unnecessary here to sketch out a program of coordinating activities in the communications and energy fields. Ample need for coordinated activities exists and the objectives are reasonably clear. Indeed, stagnation is apparent in many fields because of the lack of such coordination. In the energy field, however, emphasis should be placed upon the development of new sources of energy such as the hydrogenation of coal and oil-bearing rocks and also upon the wider employment of atomic energy. In the light of our dwindling water resources the need for energy to distill fresh water from the sea to make our arid areas fertile, is a commanding objective—a new frontier of untold significance to us and the world.

F. RELATIONSHIP OF THE AGENCIES TO THE EXECUTIVE AND THE LEGISLATIVE

Some of the relationships of the agencies to the President have been sketched out in the preceding sections of this Report. The policy planning of those agencies engaged in the areas of transportation, communications and energy, respectively, would be geared to the President as indicated through the offices to be established in the Executive Office. These offices concern the coordination of policy.

The development of detailed plans for the reorganization of the administrative agencies and continued oversight of these activities remains to be considered. Such oversight as is exercised by the Bureau of the Budget is at too low a level and extends substantially only to managerial functioning. The areas in which the agencies fail or hesitate to formulate policy presently tend to go unnoticed as do those overlaps that have developed or are in formulation.

Congestion of dockets, time-consuming procedures, duplication of facilities and effort, and failures to delegate run-of-the-mine problems all have to be watched. This function of the President must be focused somewhere. The Bureau of the Budget is not the appropriate place. A hostility inevitably arises between the Bureau of the Budget and the agencies from the very existence of the Bureau as the watch dog of potential expenditures. What is needed is the development of an urge for adequate reorganization on the part of the agencies before the Bureau of the Budget, the President and the Congress. The person charged with these responsibilities should not be a mere Inspector-General but also a source of imaginative and creative activity. Lodging that function in the Executive Office of the President independently of the Budget and transferring to that office the functions now exercised by the Bureau of the Budget of managerial assistance is the solution.

Presidential concern, with the work of the agencies, is important both from the standpoint of the President's duty to see that the laws are faithfully executed and from the standpoint of the morale of the agencies for they will then realize how important their activities are to the national scene. To neglect these agencies is to encourage the centrifugal tendencies inherent in the "administrative branch" of the government and to lessen their capacity to draw good men into their service.

Their relationship to the Congress would similarly be improved by the suggestions heretofore made. Congress will still have to concern itself with innumerable details, for details are the grist of the legislative mill. But in exercising its general functions of oversight, the function that President Wilson termed one of the most important of the duties of the Congress, the woods are often obscured by the trees. This is inevitable if the general design of the activity of these agencies is obscured, for then their operations are viewed in a fragmentized fashion by the various different committees and subcommittees of the Congress. It is the design that is of prime importance to the Committees on Government Operations and that design will be far more clearly and effectively comprehended if the suggestions heretofore made are carried out.

One matter needs further comment. The fact that the Executive Office of the President will play a large part in the architectonics of particular administrative programs should not be utilized as a basis for the claim of executive immunity from Congressional scrutiny. The establishment of national goals to be effective must involve, as President Roosevelt so aptly observed, teamwork between the Executive and the Legislative. That teamwork should carry down to all levels. Weaknesses in planning or in the execution of plans are a matter of broad public concern and the Congress has its duty to discover and divulge these weaknesses, assess the blame for their occurrences, and assist in making such provisions as it can for their cure.

SUMMARY AND CONCLUSIONS

A number of suggestions with reference to improving the organization and procedures of certain of the regulatory agencies are contained in the above report. Many of these recommendations can be adopted, if deemed desirable, by action of the agencies themselves; others can be incorporated in the plans for reorganization to be prepared as suggested below and are therefore not repeated in this summary.

But there are certain matters that need immediate attenion, such as administrative delays and the lack of policy formulation both within an agency and among various agencies. An answer that can be made to the co-ordination of inter-agency activities is the consolidation of their various functions within a new Department. Such an answer may eventually be the right answer to many of the situations herein detailed. It was the answer made in 1953 by the creation in the Department of Health, Education and Welfare and the consolidation within it of functions formerly widely dispersed. But the beginnings of that project go back thirty years to a recommendation by President Harding in 1923. The present needs are too pressing to await the initiation of what would be a mammoth project of consolidation in the fields of transportation, communication, and energy, and even a huge project in any one of them. The prime and immediate need in these fields is for developing and coordinating policy immediately at a high staff level. Operations for the moment can be left to the existing agencies, whose conduct should in the light of these recommendations show marked improvements. If experience later would dictate the desirability of the consolidation of certain operating functions, they will then have become sufficiently identified and understood to enable their intelligent consolidation in an appropriate departmental structure. To attempt such consolidation in the absence of the experience that would be derived from determined effort to evolve policy through coordination directly under the President, would be substantially to plan *in vacuo*. The creation of a mechanism for staff coordination can and should begin now. Its staff work as envisaged herein will carry within itself means for the implementation of its directives.

With this thought in mind, the following recommendations are made:

1. Secure for the President from the Congress the right to propose reorganization plans pursuant to powers heretofore granted the President under the Reorganization Act of 1949, subject to veto by a concurrent resolution of both Houses of the Congress. The powers to propose plans should be available for a minimum of two years but preferably for four years.

2. Propose a reorganization plan for the Interstate Commerce Commission whereby its Chairman will be designated by the President and serve as Chairman at his pleasure.

3. Propose a reorganization plan for the Federal Power Commission making clear that the tenure of its Chairman is at the pleasure of the President.

4. Propose reorganization plans for the Interstate Commerce Commission, the Civil Aeronautics Board, the Federal Communications Commission, the Federal Power Commission, the National Labor Relations Board, the Federal Trade Commission, and the Securities

and Exchange Commission which will make clear that the Chairman's authority extends to all administrative matters within the agency, including responsibility for the preparation and review of its budget estimates, the distribution of appropriated funds according to major programs and purposes, and the appointment of all personnel, except (i) those whose appointment is by statute vested in the President, (ii) division heads whose appointment must be confirmed by a majority of the agency members, (iii) special assistants, not in excess of three, to each of the members, which appointments shall be made by the respective members.

5. Propose reorganization plans for the same agencies providing for the delegation to panels of agency members, single agency members, hearing examiners or boards of employees for final determination all adjudicatory matters subject only to discretionary review by the agency *en banc* on petition by a party in interest.

6. Create within the Executive Office of the President with appropriate powers an office for the Coordination and Development of Transportation Policy to develop and implement a national transportation policy. This should be accomplished by a reorganization plan transferring to this Office all the responsibilities now vested in the Undersecretary of Commerce for Transportation.

7. Create within the Executive Office of the President with appropriate powers an Office for the Coordination and Development of Communications Policy and simultaneously by executive order transfer to this Office all powers relating to telecommunications now vested in the Office of Civil and Defense Mobilization.

8. Create within the Executive Office of the President with appropriate powers an Office for the Coordination and Development of Energy Policy with authority to propose to the President plans for the development of the energy resources of this nation.

9. Create within the Executive Office of the President with appropriate powers an Office for the Oversight of Regulatory Agencies which will assist the President in discharging his responsibility of assuring the efficient execution of those laws that these agencies administer.

10. Abolish the present President's Advisory Committee on Government Organization.

11. Abolish the positions of such Special Assistants to the President who have heretofore had as their major concern matters within the purview of the Offices to be created under recommendations 6, 7, 8 and 9.

12. The offices mentioned in recommendations 6, 7, 8 and 9 can be substituted for the Office for Emergency Management, which in its present form can be abolished.

13. Impose upon the Office for the Oversight of Regulatory Agencies the duty to prepare for the President detailed reorganization plans for the regulatory agencies with prime emphasis on the Federal Power Commission, the Interstate Commerce Commission, the Civil Aeronautics Board, and the Federal Communications Commission.

14. Issue an Executive Order dealing with the ethics of government employees and their duty to reject and refrain from receiving *ex parte* presentations in pending matters before them for adjudication on the record, which Order should specifically prohibit any such *ex parte* communication by any person in or part of the offices created under recommendations 6, 7, 8 and 9.

15. Promote the organization of the Administrative Conference of the United States and subject to the approval of its by-laws initially by executive order and subsequently by legislation provide for the creation of a Secretariat to the Conference, transferring to that Secretariat duties now performed by the Office of Administrative Procedure within the Department of Justice, which would thus be abolished and transferring from the Civil Service Commission to the Secretariat duties now exercised by the Commission with respect to the qualifications and grading of hearing examiners.

16. Require the submission to the Congress and President of annual reports by the offices created pursuant to recommendations 6, 7, 8 and 9.

9: YOUTH SERVICE FRONTIERS

The problem is to devise a new government instrument which can help match the apparent needs of the underdeveloped countries for trained manpower with the swelling supply of dedicated American young people eager to participate in constructive activities in the underdeveloped countries. Such an instrument should be in a position to experiment with a variety of kinds of programs, since we do not know enough about how best to operate them to launch with confidence a massive unified program. On the other hand it is important that these programs should be coordinated both with each other and with the entire range of U.S. technical assistance activities and that they should all come under a common symbolic heading.

The proposed solution is the establishment of a new agency, the International Youth Service Agency, with a director reporting to the director or coordinator of U.S. development assistance programs and a distinguished board representative of the major private groups with experience and interest in the employment of young people overseas. The Agency (IYSA) would operate mainly through contracts or grants to a variety of private non-profit organizations such as universities. It would establish standards for the operation of approved programs, to be called International Youth Service Programs, but would not itself administer programs in the field. It would develop information on the precise characteristics of manpower needs and the availability of young people to meet them, provide technical assistance to approved programs in matters of selection, training, administration overseas, relations with foreign governments and institutions and the like. It would provide funds for administration, training, transportation, and supplement to the salaries of members of IYS programs, though they would be paid local salaries in foreign countries by the host institutions. It would conduct, in house or by contract, an extensive program of research and evaluation on the entire range of approved IYS programs.

The program should be launched on a limited pilot basis with no

Submitted by Dr. Max Millikan, director of the Center for International Studies at the Massachusetts Institute of Technology.

more than a few hundred members employed on tasks now known to be clearly vital to the recipient countries. It would be expanded as experience with the various pilot ventures yielded confidence in the criteria which should be applied. Tough criteria of both academic and personality qualifications should be required by IYSA; participants should be required to commit themselves for at least two years, and should all have at least a bachelor's degree. Some programs should be developed for those with graduate degrees in such professional fields as agriculture, medicine, engineering, and the like.

It is my recommendation that at this stage no selective service exemption should be granted to participants in this program but that individual participants should be eligible for consideration for deferment in the same way that some graduate students in the United States are allowed to continue their studies.

Rationale of International Youth Service

The appropriate rationale for an International Youth Service is suggested by two key phenomena which have been emerging with increasing clarity in recent months.

The first of these is that many of the underdeveloped countries engaged in active programs of modernizing their political, social and economic life confront over the next two or three decades serious shortages of educated and trained people to carry out programs of education, improvement of health, reform of agriculture, promotion of industry, improvements of government administration, expansion of technical training, development of programs of social welfare and community development, and the like. Most of these countries are developing plans for the training of suitable numbers of their own citizens to fulfill these functions but because training and education are inherently slow processes with long lead times the flow of indigenous personnel will be grossly inadequate in the early years.

This gap in available skills could be at least partially filled and the modernization of these societies, so critical to their stability, accelerated if they could make use of substantial numbers of people from developed countries. The needs vary from one underdeveloped country to another, but in almost all there will be for at least the next decade serious shortages of trained people at all levels of education and experience. Preliminary studies in a few of these countries have established clearly that a part of this need could be met by young people with the equivalent of bachelor's or master's degrees in a wide variety of different fields.

The second fact supported by a mounting flow of incontestable evidence is that there are large and growing numbers of Americans in their twenties deeply motivated to place their energies and talents at the service of constructive world causes and prepared to devote two or three years of their lives to such services irrespective of their long-term career objectives. This motivation is growing in all sections of the American public, but it is particularly noticeable among students currently engaged in undergraduate and graduate training.

If the need of the underdeveloped countries for the services of trained young people and the supply of young persons dedicated to international service can be effectively matched, a number of important purposes of U.S. national policy can be served. Some of these are:

1. The economic and social modernization of the underdeveloped world under free institutions can be considerably accelerated. That this is a vital U.S. interest because of its contribution to a peaceful and orderly international community is a fundamental premise of current American foreign policy.

2. By this means a better understanding by the peoples of the underdeveloped countries of American institutions and of the purposes, values, and motivations of Americans can be brought about. There is abundant evidence that this kind of understanding is more effectively promoted by the engagement of individual Americans and foreigners on joint efforts to solve common problems than by massive propaganda or information programs, though these have their place. It must of course be said that such joint efforts if improperly conceived and poorly administered can backfire badly and damage rather than improve international understanding, but these risks, some of which are elaborated later in this report, can be minimized.

3. A program of this kind can play an important part in building over time a growing reservoir of American citizens with an intimate knowledge and understanding of conditions in other parts of the world. As the world becomes increasingly interdependent such a reservoir is important, first, to provide nuclei of informed public support for American foreign policy, and, second, to provide a pool of people from which more mature individuals can be drawn for later overseas service, public and private, in the American interest.

4. Such a program can provide a challenge and an outlet for the deep

desire of Americans to find, in the American tradition, new and constructive opportunities for expressing their most deeply held values.

PRINCIPALS TO GUIDE A U.S. INTERNATIONAL YOUTH SERVICE

1. The members of such a service must be selected with a view to their being capable of effectively filling locally felt needs for trained manpower in the underdeveloped countries. If the members of such a service are not felt by the host country to be genuinely helpful and useful in promoting that country's own objectives, the program, whatever its educational benefits for the Americans involved, will create frictions which will frustrate American purposes. There are currently in operation a number of privately sponsored programs for sending young people overseas with the primary purpose of contributing to their education and understanding of foreign countries, such as the "Experiment in International Living," "Operation Crossroads Africa," and the like. These serve a very useful purpose and deserve encouragement, but their contribution to solving the manpower problems of the host countries is not sufficient to justify their inclusion, at least in the initial stages, in a program financed by the U.S. government. A central criterion for International Youth Service activities must be their demonstrable utility to public or private institutions in the host country.

2. A corollary of this first principle is that the International Youth Service should be conceived as an integral part of the broader U.S. government effort to assist the underdeveloped countries in building the institutions essential to self-confident and effective nationhood. ICA, the U.S. government agency up to now responsible for technical assistance, has for the most part confined its activities in the past to the provision of technically qualified advisors to the underdeveloped countries. The International Youth Service will be much more effective if it is part of a broader effort by the ICA or a successor nation-building agency to provide assistance to the underdeveloped countries in meeting their operational manpower needs during the period when a gap exists between those needs and the supply of indigenous trained people to meet them. Some efforts have already been launched by ICA to cooperate with the underdeveloped countries in estimating their trained manpower requirements over a future period. These efforts should be greatly expanded and in particular should be focused on the qualifications required of foreign personnel who might be supplied to fill the gaps at all levels in the indigenous

manpower supply. Such surveys will provide a much sounder base for estimating the character and extent of that portion of the needs which might be filled by relatively young college graduates.

3. While these surveys, to be conducted at the initiative of the host governments but with the assistance of the United States and other developed countries, are essential to the development over time of maximum effectiveness in the International Youth Service, its inauguration on a pilot basis need not await their conclusion. Some surveys of these needs have already been made in some countries which establish the probable utility of significant numbers of young Americans. For example, the so-called Ashby Commission in Nigeria has estimated the maximum requirement for secondary school teachers in that country over the next twenty years, the probably minimum supply of Nigerians to fill these posts, and the gap which might be filled by foreign personnel. The Commission believes that young Americans and Western Europeans with college degrees could, with some additional training, be effectively employed in these posts. In a number of other cases minimal needs are apparent to informed observers even in the absence of careful surveys. The Colorado State University study of the Point Four Youth Corps now in progress under a contract from ICA will identify some of these presently apparent needs which might be served by an International Youth Service.

It might be noted that in few if any of the underdeveloped countries do these needs include relatively unskilled manual labor, for which there is in most cases a surplus indigenous supply. Thus the program could be started on a pilot basis with certain activities where it is already clear that there would not only be no competition between foreign members of an International Youth Service and citizens of the host country but where the manpower supplied from outside can fill a crucial requirement that cannot be met in any other way. As the surveys proposed in paragraph 2 above are completed, additional areas of need can be clearly identified and the Youth Service expanded to meet them.

4. It is probable that many different kinds of programs to employ youth abroad, with many different standards and characteristics, will be needed and desirable. A substantial number of private agencies are already administering small programs of this kind. Others are in process of formation. Since the needs are various and unclear, the experience with such programs to date is too limited to give us confidence that we know precisely how they should be designed, a

large amount of experimentation is called for in the early years of the program. This suggests that a massive, centralized, federally operated program is not the right way to launch this effort. Rather, it is suggested that a small semi-autonomous government organization should be established which we shall refer to hereafter as the International Youth Service Agency, which would operate mainly through contracts with or grants to a variety of different privately organized programs. The structure and functions of the IYSA will be described later, but broadly it would provide information to and coordinate private activities, establish standards to be met by programs to be certified as International Youth Service Programs, provide funds for the support of certain of the activities of such programs, provide technical assistance to such programs in matters of organization, selection, training, overseas administration, relations with foreign governments, institutions, and the like, and conduct either directly or by contrast an extensive program of research and evaluation. To be eligible for financial aid and for certification as an International Youth Service activity, private groups would be required to meet the standards laid down by the IYSA. The nature of these standards is described later.

5. Especially in the early stages the standards of training and selection imposed by the IYSA should be very high. A few dramatic failures in the early pilot stages could do irreparable harm to the program as a whole. The enthusiasm for such programs among the youth of the country and the numbers of persons eager to participate even under relatively difficult conditions are believed to be such that the IYSA can afford to be very highly selective without risking a supply of participants more than enough to meet the numbers that can be effectively placed and administered in the early years. At least at the beginning, the level of training and maturity that goes with an undergraduate college degree should be a minimum. A number of programs for persons with various kinds of graduate degrees should be actively explored.

6. International Youth Service Programs should be explicitly designed to fill a temporary shortage of indigenous persons with the necessary qualifications in the host country. Such programs should be accompanied by and integrated with programs developed by ICA or its successor agency for the training of adequate numbers of host country citizens to take over in due course the functions to be performed in the interim by IYS programs. Such programs should in every case be an integral part of broader programs worked out

between the host country and technical assistance agencies of the
United States, foreign countries, or international bodies for filling
the long-run manpower and institutional requirements of the host
country. Such programs will include many elements not within the
purview of IYSA such as the bringing of citizens of the host countries
to the United States and other developed countries for training,
support to the indigenous institutions of the host country, etc.

7. Members of the International Youth Service will normally
serve in operational rather than advisory capacities in the foreign
country. This means that unlike technical assistance personnel who
are employees of the U.S. government assigned to assist foreign
organizations, members of the IYS should normally be employed by
and responsible to institutions in the foreign country. They will be
serving in a kind of internship rather than as technical advisors.
Clearly the terms and conditions of their employment must be worked
out cooperatively between the sponsoring U.S. organization and the
institution or agency in the recipient country with very considerable
care to avoid possible conflict and controversy. For each such program there should probably be established a high level board with
responsible representatives of both the host country or institution
and the sponsoring organization. This will require delicate and
careful negotiation and administration. Where possible, primary
responsibility for this should rest with the private American institution sponsoring the program but with advice and assistance from
both the IYSA in Washington and the U.S. Technical Cooperation
Mission in the field. It is essential however for the smooth working
of the program that the host institution in the foreign country should
feel that IYS members are their men for whom they are basically
responsible and over whom they have at least partial control. Much
more careful thought should be given to the pattern of these arrangements.

8. In line with the principle set forth in the preceding paragraph,
it will probably normally be desirable that the host country institution accept the obligation to pay IYS members salaries in local
currency at the rate applicable for jobs of the kinds they hold.
Their willingness to do this will be an important index of the value
to them of the functions being performed by IYS members. Certain
costs will clearly have to be paid out of funds appropriated by the
Congress to IYSA. These will include costs of training, maintenance,
and salary while outside the host country, costs of transportation
from the United States, costs of medical treatment and medical

insurance over and above what the host country provides, and the like. In cases where the host country salary scale is low salary supplements can be provided from IYSA funds particularly for people with higher levels of professional training. This must be handled, however, with very great care to avoid the appearance in the host country of a significantly different standard of living for foreign than for indigenous personnel. The sense of dedication of those applying for the youth corps should be such that they are prepared to accept standards of remuneration substantially lower than those they could expect from jobs in the United States. This question likewise requires much more thorough study.

9. One of the most important and difficult problems of administrating a program of this kind is provision for adequate administration and supervision of the activities of IYS members by mature and responsible Americans. While as suggested above IYS members should essentially be working for the host country institution, there must be for each small group of American IYS members a senior responsible American in the host country to follow their activities in detail. In the case of the larger programs these team leaders can perhaps be supplied by the sponsoring American organization. In these cases the IYSA must establish standards and criteria for American supervision and provide assistance in arranging for it. In other cases such supervision might be supplied by senior people assigned by ICA to technical assistance missions in the host country.

Supervision of this kind will probably be best handled by people who have been sent to the host country to do jobs in education, agriculture, medicine, or some other field in which the IYSA is operating and to take on this supervisory task as an additional responsibility. It should be remembered that such supervision will call for administrative and diplomatic talents of the highest order. Further study and experimentation on this problem of American supervision of IYS members in the field is certainly urgently needed.

10. One of the most important standards to be set by IYSA for approved programs has to do with the character and extent of the special training to be provided the participants in such programs before they take up their duties in the foreign country. Here again considerable experimentation is called for and a variety of training schemes should be tried. However, certain basic conditions should be established for all such schemes.

In virtually all cases a minimum of several months of training will almost certainly be wise. This should include some rudimentary language instruction in the native language of the area to which participants are to be assigned. For work in regions in which a European language other than English is for historical reasons the lingua franca, notably French and Spanish, candidates for assignment to those areas should probably have some competence in the European language as a condition for selection. For language training in native dialects it may be possible to use as instructors students from the areas in question resident in the United States. This has the added virtue of making the International Youth Service concept applicable in a mutual two-way fashion rather than as a unilateral matter. This point is elaborated in paragraph 18 below. In addition, there must be instruction in the economic, cultural, social, and political characteristics of the region to which the participant will be assigned. There should also be some instruction in the special circumstances of application of the professional field in which the candidate will be working, e.g., education, health, agriculture, industry, etc.

For the larger programs, especially those sponsored by educational institutions, the sponsoring organization may take on responsibility for performing the training function according to standards established by IYSA. In other cases where it appears desirable, IYSA may take separate training contracts with educational institutions to conduct the training required for the program in the United States for the benefit of a number of sponsoring organizations. As the training requirements for those programs are clarified, IYSA may be able to distribute to educational institutions information on the kinds of course work which it might be desirable for candidates to try to work into their regular academic programs in advance of making application for membership in the International Youth Service. What fraction of the prerequisites can be assured by selection and what fraction must be supplied by training after selection will have to be determined experimentally as the program proceeds. In many cases it may be desirable to establish an additional training and orientation period in the foreign country before the participant actually starts his internship activities.

11. Another set of standards which must be established by IYSA relate to the procedures for the selection of participants. Professional and academic qualifications are certainly important here, but maturity, personality characteristics, flexibility and adaptability, and capacity to adjust to difficult living conditions are all important. Unfortunately, the science of testing for these intangibles is still quite primitive. We do not yet have formal tests which can substitute for the wise

intuitions of experienced interviewers. The judgment of those organizations which already have some experience in the selection of people for overseas assignments should be drawn on heavily here. This is one of the areas to which serious research attention should be given by IYSA as recommended in the next paragraph.

12. Throughout the above comments it has been emphasized that this must be an experimental program. This underlines the importance of building into the program from the beginning procedures for the evaluation of alternative modes of organization, methods of selection and training, relations with foreign governments and institutions, and the like. A condition for each program to be sponsored by IYSA should be an adequate plan by the sponsoring organization for the evaluation of its own procedures. In addition, IYSA should have funds to finance independent contracts for research and evaluation of all of its aspects.

13. It is difficult to estimate the numbers of young people that might effectively be utilized in programs of this sort. Because of the experimental nature of the program, and the limited information now available about needs, it should certainly be started on a small scale. In view of the number of private activities which have already accumulated some experience, it should probably be possible to place several hundred young people in the first year or two, but there should be no pressure to achieve greater volume until there is sufficient experience and background study to give some confidence that expanded numbers can be wisely used. The possible rate of expansion will depend in considerable measure on the extent to which studies of the over-all manpower demand and supply situation can be promoted by ICA or its successor agency.

14. Another reason for starting modestly is that it is highly desirable that members of the Youth Service be spread in small numbers through the host society. It would be unfortunate if the service led to the establishment of substantial American communities in the foreign country not easily assimilated into the local society. This would greatly reduce both the educational value of the program to the participant and its service value to the host country as well as posing serious positive dangers of the kind illustrated by American enclaves of military and other personnel abroad. There will be a temptation to assemble groups of youth corps members together because of the ease of administration and supervision but this must be vigorously resisted.

15. There should be experimentation with the most suitable term

of service, as with other aspects of the program, but particularly
in the early stages it would appear undesirable to support programs
of less than two years duration (including the training period).

16. As to age limits, it seems most unlikely that programs of the
kind here envisaged can be operated effectively with people under
twenty-one and even in this age group, general maturity should be
an important principle of selection. While the needs of the underdeveloped countries are for people of all mature age groups and it is
hoped that the U.S. nation-building agency will develop more effective
procedures than it now has for recruiting people in mid-career, there
is an important symbolic value in treating the International Youth
Service as a separate piece of the assistance program designed primarily for people just coming out of undergraduate and graduate
schools.

17. On the controversial matter of the selective service status of
members of the International Youth Service, it is my view that it
would be undesirable to publicize this program as an alternative to
the draft. The numbers will certainly be small in the early years and
there is abundant evidence that draft exemption is not required as
a bait to induce an adequate number of applications to permit
the selection of a first-class group. It would of course be desirable to
prevent the disruption of the program which would be caused by IYS
members being subject to draft call while on duty with the Service.
It would be desirable therefore for authority to be provided for deferment of individuals in the service on much the same basis as defer-
ments are granted to students in the United States taking graduate
training.

18. The International Youth Service Agency should give serious
study to a variety of possible ways of giving the program a two-way
character by exploring possible services to be performed in the United
States by young people sent here for education and training from the
underdeveloped countries. A certain amount of this now goes on in
informal ways. Local communities call upon foreign students for
lectures, discussion groups, occasional language instruction, and the
like. Systematic examination might well reveal a substantially expanded set of possibilities for part-time activity of this sort. The
most promising areas would appear to be participation by foreign
students in the United States' primary and secondary school system
in course work designed to introduce the students to economic,
cultural, political, and geographic conditions in the underdeveloped
countries. They might perform services in more advanced educational

programs at the college level including perhaps language instruction. They might as suggested above be utilized for these purposes in the training programs of the International Youth Service activity.

They might be used in some adult education activities in the United States, though there are dangers to their own development in having them placed in the position with adult groups of having to explain or defend the foreign policies of their governments. In any case, the values of trying to give the Youth Service idea a genuinely international flavor with real elements of reciprocity are so great that these possibilities should be very seriously explored.

ORGANIZATIONAL STRUCTURE

1. What is here proposed is that there be established by Congressional action an International Youth Service Agency. There are virtues in giving such a body semi-autonomous status and freeing it from the bureaucratic rigidities of the Civil Service and of regular government departments. On the other hand, it is absolutely essential that this activity be closer coordinated with and indeed be an integral part of the U.S. government's nation-building activities. On balance, my present feeling is that the virtues of having it report to the director of the U.S. foreign aid program outweigh the disadvantages of this solution.

2. It should be headed by a director of international stature, probably from the academic world but with great knowledge of the underdeveloped countries and with unusual administrative and diplomatic skills.

3. To underline its semi-autonomous status, it should be governed by a board of directors on which should sit representatives from ICA, USIA, the State Department, the major foundations, representatives of the principal professions in which the Service is active (education, health, agriculture, etc.) and at least one senior social scientist distinguished for his work on underdeveloped areas.

4. It should have a small staff of its own but should in addition rely heavily for information and advice on the staff of the ICA. It should utilize studies of manpower needs of that organization and coordinate closely with its technical assistance and institution building activities.

5. It should directly administer no overseas Youth Service programs itself, but should have funds to encourage and support by contracts and grants-in-aid a wide variety of such programs conducted by private organizations.

6. Its functions should include the following:

a. To develop information on the one hand on needs for manpower in the underdeveloped areas which might be met by young persons with undergraduate or graduate training and on the other hand on the availability throughout the United States to young people with suitable skills to meet these needs.

b. To establish standards for programs to be certified as approved International Youth Service Programs including standards for: selection and qualifications for personnel, training, administration in the field, period of service, salary and prerequisites of members, minimum health safeguards, evaluation.

c. To finance, in part or in whole, by contract or grant-in-aid, approved programs to be administered by private nonprofit organizations, such financing to include provision for administration, training, transportation, medical care and insurance, and in some instances salary supplements.

d. To arrange for and finance training programs for IYS members.

e. To act as a clearing house to provide information and assistance to universities, foundations, and other nonprofit private organizations on all aspects of International Youth Service programs.

f. To stimulate the development of new programs by suitable institutions and organizations in areas where there is a demonstrable need not yet met by existing programs.

g. To sponsor independent research and evaluation of alternative methods and procedures for conducting such programs.

CONCLUSIONS

The key concept of this proposal is that particularly in its early stages this should be an experimental program in which the IYSA would support a wide variety of schemes having in common that they are devices to use young Americans in filling the interim manpower needs of the underdeveloped countries while they are expanding their own human resources. The danger and risks to which such a program is exposed should not be underestimated. The whole program could be brought into irreparable disrepute in the early stages if it is started on too ambitious a scale, if it pays too little attention to careful selection of the participants, if the approved programs take insufficient account of the nature of the needs of the underdeveloped countries, if they are conducted with inadequate awareness of the subtle and difficult problems of retaining good relations with the officials and institutions of the foreign countries or if they exercise inadequate firmness in insisting with host government and institutions on conditions which give the program a chance of success.

On the other hand, too great caution and rigidity in the administration of the program could be equally bad. It should be recognized from the beginning that there will inevitably be some failures and some mistakes. These will not be fatal if they are limited to parts of the program and counterbalanced by some notable successes. It is essentially for this reason that we recommend a variety of differing contracts with private organizations each of which will bear principal responsibility for its own program rather than a massive centrally organized governmental effort. The fact is that we simply do not know a great deal about how to make a program of this kind a success. Sensible administration can, by setting minimum standards, avoid gross and predictable errors but the administration must be bold and flexible in trying a variety of arrangements to test the best methods. The program should be undertaken in the conviction that it must be possible to find a sensible way of matching the undoubted enthusiasm and dedication of the young people of the United States for international service with the equally undoubted manpower needs of the underdeveloped countries.

10: CULTURAL FRONTIERS

A unified and purposeful effort in educational, cultural, technical, scientific and informational cooperation programs is essential to our foreign policy objective of the achievement of peace through the extension of knowledge and understanding in the world.

To create a national effort with purpose and thrust requires first of all, strong Presidential leadership in four directions (a) in keeping this part of our foreign relations uppermost in the minds of the American people; (b) in securing legislation appropriations from the Congress; (c) in insisting upon more coordinated and effective work within the Executive Branch; and (d) in assuring other nations of our continuing unequivocal engagement with them in world-wide educational, cultural, scientific and technical development.

This kind of effective action by government is achieved through the establishment of an "action center," that is, a post which is given sufficient backing by the President and his cabinet to activate, stimulate and coordinate varied programs in different governmental departments and agencies. By virtue of the signal importance given this position in the achievement of far-reaching national objectives, it should be possible to find a person of real stature — imaginative, thoughtful and capable — to take such a position.

This "strong position" could be established in the Department of State, as an Undersecretary (or Deputy Undersecretary) of State for Educational and Cultural Affairs, or it could be set up in the Executive Office of the President, as an Executive Assistant for International Educational and Cultural Affairs. For many reasons, including our awareness of the great interest of the incoming Secretary of State in this area, we favor placing it in the Department of State, in line with the first alternative offered above.

If established as an Undersecretary (or Deputy Undersecretary) of State for Educational and Cultural Affairs, we *caution against* perpetuation of the present arrangement in which the Special Assistant to the Secretary of State for the Coordination of International Educa-

---

Prepared by a task force headed by Prof. James Davis of the University of Michigan, and including Walter Laves, William W. Marvel, Frederick D. Patterson, Calvin Pimpton, and F. Champion Ward.

tional and Cultural Relations is both the operating head of the Bureau of Educational and Cultural Affairs in the Department of State and the officer who is expected to coordinate all government programs operating through many different departments and agencies (e.g., State, ICA, USIA, HEW, Agriculture, etc.). It is our observation that this officer could not coordinate other departments while heading the operations of one department, and that he had insufficient power to coordinate. He was unable to coordinate effectively programs outside his own department unless the agency operating them chose to be coordinated.

In order to give strength to the coordinated educational, technical and cultural exchange program of the United States, we recommend the creation of a new *Advisory Commission on Educational Exchange*. The new Commission would advise the new Undersecretary.

This Presidentially-appointed citizen body can most easily be established through legislation to amend P.L. 402 which created the existing U.S. Advisory Commission on Educational Exchange. The amendment should

a. broaden the scope of the Commission to include the full spectrum of educational exchange and development, with special reference to the establishment of mutually fruitful relations with the private agencies;

b. expand the membership from five to nine in order to get a more representative group of persons who have knowledge of and experience in the varied operations of exchange and development programs in the U.S. and abroad: the requirement that they have particular political party affiliations should be eliminated;

c. give authority for the Commission to assemble ad hoc consultant panels for short-term consideration of particular programs, with a member of the Commission serving as chairman of each of the panels so convened (and, in appropriations legislation, provide funds for the operation of these consultant panels); and

d. authorize an adequate staff for the Commission.

If Presidential leadership is provided, and a strong action position is established and well filled, then the specific operational proposals which we see as of real importance to the success of the program can be dealt with. Among the specific recommendations suggested, we call particular attention to the first.

We recommend that the President request of the Bureau of the Budget immediate action toward utilizing for international educational and cultural purposes more foreign currency accumulated from agricultural sales and loans. These holdings constitute a capital asset of the American people through which should be created a *Mutual Educational and Cultural Cooperation Fund.*

Combined with increased dollar appropriations, the foreign currency holdings would provide ample funds for local expenditures in many of the principal areas of the world where educational and cultural development programs are most in need of expansion. The funds could be used to assist financing, not only of U.S. Government programs but of U.S. university and other private educational programs abroad (university-to-university programs, graduate area-study centers abroad, student and "youth corps" activities, etc., etc.

Therefore, we recommend that departments and agencies of government conducting educational, cultural and technical and cooperation programs (State, ICA, USIA, Agriculture, HEW, etc.) be requested immediately to submit to the Department of State program proposals to be financed from these foreign currencies, making maximum cooperative use of private agencies to provide program services.

These foreign currencies are not available in some parts of the world most in need of assistance, such as Africa, for example, and accompanying dollar expenditures are necessary to support their most effective use. Thus, we recommend that departments and agencies of government conducting educational, cultural and technical cooperation programs (as noted above) be requested immediately to submit supplemental dollar proposals for FY 1962 for programs urgently needed and now excluded from the budget request to be submitted by President Eisenhower.

Action needed to implement this recommendation is: (1) President's order to Bureau of the Budget. (2) President's request to agencies for program proposals using foreign currency. (3) President's request to agencies for supplemental dollar proposals. (4) President's support of supplemental dollar proposals in Budget Bureau and in Congress.

Educational institutions, foundations and other private agencies now carry the largest part of the total American program of educational and cultural cooperation. Their direct services to students and visitors are the "cutting edge" of the program. They are increasingly pressed to expand their services to American students and others. There is a desperate need for more dollars to strengthen these institutions so that they may improve and expand their indispensable contributions.

New appropriations must be authorized. They could be administered either by the Department of State, and by other governmental agencies, or through a new government-aided foundation especially established for this purpose.

Therefore, we recommend legislation to

a. Authorize matching grants to universities and colleges, for counseling, orientation to American life, English language training, and other assistance to foreign students, 90% of whom are not sponsored nor financed by the U.S. Government. (This same proposal was embodied in S. 3058 which was introduced by Senator Fulbright and supported by Senator Kennedy, passed by the Senate of the 86th Congress, 2nd session, but not reported for vote by the House.);

b. Authorize matching grants to local organizations for direct expenses incurred in programming sizeable numbers of U.S. Government-sponsored short-term foreign visiting leaders and specialists;

c. Reimburse the educational institutions (on the pattern of the original G.I. Bill) for the real costs of educating U.S. government-sponsored foreign students and ICA participants, to the extent that these costs exceed normal tuition fees;

d. Provide funds to universities, colleges, and other selected organizations for emergency assistance to superior non-government sponsored foreign students to help them reach a nearly-attained academic objective (along the lines of the precedent established through the former Chinese Student Emergency Aid Program from 1950 to 1954); and

e. Provide funds to universities to enable them to bring foreign visiting scholars and graduate students for teaching, research and study (e.g., either in order to bring strategic individuals who might not accept a direct U.S. Government grant, or to help them replace a faculty member released for service in a less developed country with one from a more highly developed country.)

Action needed to implement this recommendation is:

Legislation, either directing the Secretary of State or creating a new government-aided foundation especially established, to administer:

a. matching grants to universities for special services to foreign students;

b. matching grants to local organizations for special expenses for programming government-sponsored short-term visitors;

c. funds to reimburse universities for the real costs of educating government-sponsored foreign students and ICA participants;

d. grants to universities and other selected organizations for emergency assistance to superior foreign students; and

e. grants to enable universities to bring selected foreign scholars.

Agencies of government need to take seriously the minor technical irritants which inhibit the most effective operation of exchange programs and move vigorously to remedy them. We recommend that the Secretary of State undertake the revision of regulations and the proposal of new legislation, where necessary, to

a. Revise visa provisions in order to place the spouse and minor children of a foreign scholar on the same visa as he, and to extend the employment privileges of foreign scholars;

b. Change social security withholding tax provisions to exempt foreign scholars who never can achieve social security benefits; and

c. Increase and make uniform per diem stipends for living expenses for short-term foreign visitors sponsored by different government agencies.

Action needed to implement these recommendations is:

(1) Legislation to amend the Immigration and Nationality Act of 1952.

(2) Legislation to amend Social Security Law.

(3) Proposed new Undersecretary to study and recommend increase and uniformity in per diem expense stipends for sponsored foreign visitors.

The preparation of the report has led us to a number of viewpoints which we wish to state. These recommendations do not embody the immediacy and urgency criteria which we have tried to apply to the foregoing.

We do consider them worth stating. They could be *referred to the Secretary of State for implementation.*

(1) We did not spend much time studying the many proposals for implementing the "Youth Corps" because there is another task force so occupied.

In view of the large resources in many parts of the American citizenry—young people, minority groups, educators, and others—from which persons could be selected for service in less developed countries, we urge careful attention to the selection, orientation and, particularly, the supervision and use of such people to the end that their service clearly benefit the peoples toward whom it is extended.

(2) The very fruitful "Fulbright Programs" have been developed through bi-national agreements based upon the chance availability of foreign currencies. We consider this an inadequate basis for directing our national efforts for educational exchange and recommend the

development of means to extend these bi-national programs using better criteria.

(3) We recommend that agencies of government encourage partici-pation of all qualified U.S. institutions of higher education in cultural cooperation programs.

(4) In exchange with the less developed countries, give priority to the selection of people whom these countries need for the development of indigenous institutions consonant with their national development goals.

(5) Explore possibilities for the effective expansion of educational exchange and technical assistance programs through inter-govern-mental agencies; UN, OAS, etc.

(6) We recommend increasing our exchange programs with the communist-bloc European countries as quickly as satisfactory arrange-ments can be made.

(7) The long established and highly productive educational rela-tions between the U.S. and the countries of Western Europe must not be neglected in our concern for the less developed countries.

(8) Research on the method of educational, technical, and cultural exchanges should be supported by the agencies operating educational and cultural exchange programs.

11: HOUSING FRONTIERS

1. *Cabinet Status.* Provide cabinet status for all housing and urban development activities by establishing a new Department of Housing and Urban Development.

2. *Housing for Low-Income Families.* Set up an entirely new subsidy program to provide housing for low-income families, encouraging a maximum of private enterprise participation, and giving the widest discretion to local communities in choosing their housing programs, including public housing which would be continued and improved.

3. *Federal Housing Administration.* Make the necessary increase in FHA authorizations and program extensions. Also provide a liberalization in FHA terms and set up a new FHA insurance program for site development.

4. *Federal National Mortgage Association.* Provide additional funds and authorizations for both the regular secondary market program and the special assistance program. On the question of a new form of central mortgage banking facility, recommend that the Secretary study the matter, taking into consideration the results of several private studies now nearing completion.

5. *Housing for the Elderly.* Provide additional funds for the direct loan program to nonprofit corporations for housing for the elderly, and permit it to be financed as a public debt transaction rather than via the appropriation route.

6. *College Housing.* Provide additional loan funds to meet program needs at the rate of $500 million annually.

7. *Urban Renewal.* Provide a four-year authorization of approximately $650 annually, additional funds for urban planning grants, and additional relief for displaced small businesses, and generally liberalize and improve the program.

8. *Community Facilities.* Provide $750 million over a 4-year period for a system of partial grants rather than loans; broaden project eligibility; increase funds for public works advance planning and change to a grant basis; increase funds for water pollution grants along

---

Task force: Joseph P. MacMurray, Charles A. Wellman, John Barriere, Harry Held, and Robert Wood.

the lines of the Blatnik bill, and transfer from HEW to HHFA and HEW retaining enforcement powers.

9. *Mass Transit.* As an immediate step, enact a program for planning grants and $100 million for public facility loans (along the lines of the Williams bill which passed the Senate last year), and set up a Presidential Study Commission to determine future needs.

10. *Aid to Orderly Suburban Development.* Encourage orderly suburban development by providing planning grants and a limited loan fund to enable suburban communities to acquire and improve tracts of land.

11. *Research.* Provide a new expanded program of research in housing and urban development and encourage innovation and experimentation in the FHA program.

12. *Farm Housing.* Extend the present farm housing program for 4 additional years; provide $450 million additional for direct loans to "adequate" farms, an additional $10 million for contributions to help "potentially adequate" farms, and $50 million for loans and grants to improve farm sanitation and the encouragement of family-size farms.

13. *Study Commissions.* Appointment, by the Secretary of the new Department, of four Commissions for the purpose of studying and developing proposals for legislation or administrative action on: (1) standardization of mortgage instruments and foreclosures, (2) special problems of residential mortgage credit, (3) standardization of local codes, (4) tax policies of Federal, State and local governments affecting housing construction and rehabilitation.

12: INTERNATIONAL FRONTIERS

We observe today, not a victory of party but a celebration of freedom—symbolizing an end as well as a beginning—signifying renewal as well as change. For I have sworn before you and Almighty God the same solemn oath our forebears prescribed nearly a century and three-quarters ago.

The world is very different now. For man holds in his mortal hands the power to abolish all form of human poverty and to abolish all form of human life. And yet the same revolutionary beliefs for which our forebears fought are still at issue around the globe—the belief that the rights of man come not from the generosity of the state but from the hand of God.

We dare not forget today that we are the heirs of that first revolution. Let the word go forth from this time and place, to friend and foe alike, that the torch has been passed to a new generation of Americans—born in this century, tempered by war, disciplined by a cold and bitter peace, proud of our ancient heritage—and unwilling to witness or permit the slow undoing of those human rights to which this Nation has always been committed, and to which we are committed today.

Let every nation know, whether it wish us well or ill, that we shall pay any price, bear any burden, meet any hardship, support any friend or oppose any foe in order to assure the survival and success of liberty.

This much we pledge—and more.

To those old allies whose cultural and spiritual origins we share, we pledge the loyalty of faithful friends. United, there's little we cannot do in a host of new cooperative ventures. Divided, there is little we can do—for we dare not meet a powerful challenge at odds and split asunder.

To those new states whom we now welcome to the ranks of the free, we pledge our word that one form of colonial control shall not have passed, merely to be replaced by a far more iron tyranny. We shall not always expect to find them supporting our every view. But we shall always hope to find them strongly supporting their own freedom—and to remember that, in the past, those who foolishly sought to find power by riding on the tiger's back inevitably ended up inside.

The text of President John F. Kennedy's inaugural address.

To those peoples in the huts and villages of half the globe struggling to break the bonds of mass misery, we pledge our best efforts to help them help themselves, for whatever period is required—not because the Communists are doing it, not because we seek their votes, but because it is right. If the free society cannot help the many who are poor, it can never save the few who are rich.

To our sister republics south of our border, we offer a special pledge —to convert our good words into good deeds—in a new alliance for progress—to assist free men and free governments in casting off the chains of poverty. But this peaceful revolution of hope cannot become the prey of hostile powers. Let all our neighbors know that we shall join with them to oppose aggression or subversion anywhere in the Americas. And let every other power know that this hemisphere intends to remain the master of its own house.

To that world assembly of sovereign states, the United Nations, our last best hope in an age where the instruments of war have far outpaced the instruments of peace, we renew our pledge of support—to prevent its becoming merely a forum for invective—to strengthen its shield of the new and the weak—and to enlarge the area to which its writ may run.

Finally, to those nations who would make themselves our adversary, we offer not a pledge but a request: That both sides begin anew the quest for peace, before the dark powers of destruction unleashed by science engulf all humanity in planned or accidental self-destruction.

We dare not tempt them with weakness. For only when our arms are sufficient beyond doubt can we be certain beyond doubt that they will never be employed.

But neither can two great and powerful groups of nations take comfort from their present course—both sides overburdened by the cost of modern weapons, both rightly alarmed by the steady spread of the deadly atom, yet both racing to alter that uncertain balance of terror that stays the hand of mankind's final war.

So let us begin anew—remembering on both sides that civility is not a sign of weakness, and sincerity is always subject to proof. Let us never negotiate out of fear. But let us never fear to negotiate.

Let both sides explore what problems unite us instead of belaboring the problems that divide us.

Let both sides, for the first time, formulate serious and precise proposals for the inspection and control of arms—and bring the absolute power to destroy other nations under the absolute control of all nations.

Let both sides join to invoke the wonders of science instead of its terrors. Together let us explore the stars, conquer the deserts, eradicate disease, tap the ocean depths, encourage the arts and commerce.

Let both sides be united to heed in all corners of the earth the command of Isaiah—to "undo the heavy burdens . . . (and) let the oppressed go free."

And if a beach-head of cooperation can be made in the jungles of suspicion, let both sides join in the next task: Creating, not a new balance of power, but a new world of law, where the strong are just and the weak secure and the peace preserved forever.

All this will not be finished in the first 100 days. Nor will it be finished in the first 1,000 days, in the life of this administration, nor even perhaps in our lifetime on this planet. But let us begin.

In your hands, my fellow citizens, more than in mine, will rest the final success or failure of our course. Since this country was founded, each generation has been summoned to give testimony to its national loyalty. The graves of young Americans who answered that call encircle the globe.

Now the trumpet summons us again—not as a call to bear arms, though arms we need—not as a call to battle, though embattled we are—but a call to bear the burden of a long twilight struggle, year in and year out, "rejoicing in hope, patient in tribulation"—a struggle against the common enemies of man: Tyranny, poverty, disease and war itself.

In the long history of the world, only a few generations have been granted the role of defending freedom in its hour of maximum danger. I do not shrink from this responsibility—I welcome it. I do not believe that any of us would exchange places with any other people or any other generation. The energy, the faith and the devotion which we bring to this endeavor will light our country and all who serve it—and the glow from that fire can truly light the world.

And so, my fellow Americans: Ask not what your country will do for you—ask what you can do for your country.

My fellow citizens of the world: Ask not what America will do for you, but what together we can do for the freedom of man.

Finally, whether you are citizens of America or of the world, ask of us the same high standards of strength and sacrifice that we shall ask of you. With a good conscience our only sure reward, with history the final judge of our deeds, let us go forth to lead the land we love, asking His blessing and His help, but knowing that here on earth God's work must truly be our own.

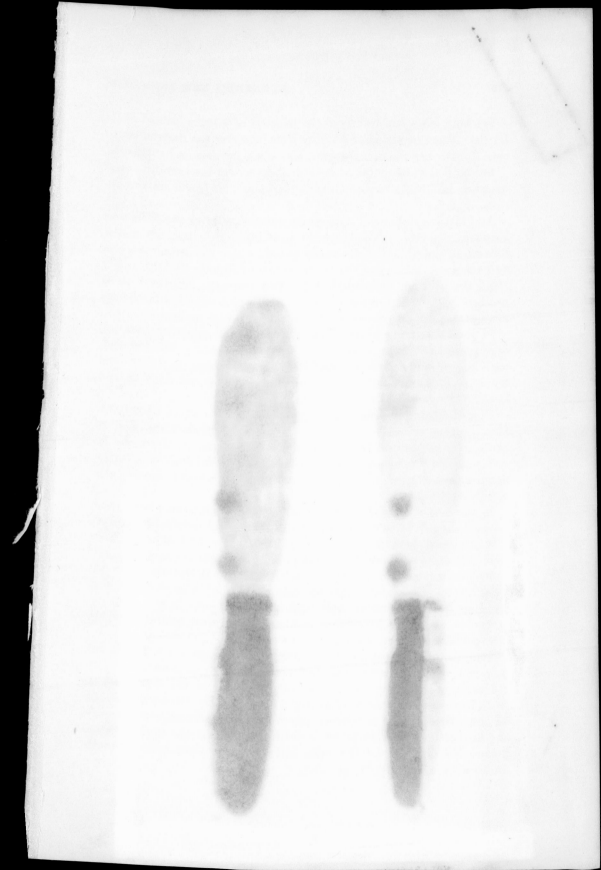

6/15/61

DATE DUE	
MAY 06 1998	

GAYLORD   PRINTED IN U.S.A.